Farming Fundamentals

Stephen A. Elich

This book is lovingly dedicated to my wife Linda for all her support, advice and encouragement.

This book was originally published in 2012 by Create Space, a division of Amazon.

About the Author
Stephen A. Elich came to the real estate industry following a career as a marketing executive for a variety of firms from Fortune 500 companies to start-ups. Acting on a passion for real estate, he earned his broker's license while working for a high-tech start-up. When the opportunity to start his real estate career presented itself, he joined Coldwell Banker in Northern California and was awarded the International President's Circle designation within three years of joining the company.

By combining his classical Marketing training and experience with the collective wisdom of long-time agents, Elich began farming early in his real estate career. He realized that the methodology he followed was something that would benefit other real estate professionals, so he wrote this book to provide a road map for other agents.

Table of Contents

Introduction

"A journey of a thousand miles begins with a single step."

— Lao-Tzu

In any given real estate office, you have a wide variety of people, each with their unique history and perspectives, but one thing remains constant – only a handful of people in the office are actually successful real estate professionals.

Why is that the case? Most people that enter the real estate business fail to understand that they are entering a career in sales. Make no mistake – if you are going to be a real estate agent, you are entering a career in sales.

The main purpose of this book is to provide those entering the business with a realistic perspective of the real estate business. This book is intended to help you with the only two things that matter in sales: 1) Prospecting for new business, and 2) Closing transactions to make money.

Farming Fundamentals is a comprehensive guide for real estate professionals who are considering farming as their primary prospecting method. Farming is a proven business development channel that has been effective for years.

Even as the real estate business is transformed by a plethora of online tools and services, many real estate practitioners are discovering that farming is more relevant than ever.

Farming today is all about enhancing traditional practices that have been vetted for years with emerging tools and services that help you sign more listing agreements.

This book is designed to give new agents a road map for success, and to supplement the knowledge of experienced agents who haven't considered farming seriously in the past. The book is composed of four sections:

Part 1 – Prospecting for Business – Farming is one of many prospecting channels available. This section provides an overview of farming and makes the case that it is the most effective and sustainable prospecting method available to real estate agents.

Part 2 – The Farm Evaluation Process – This section takes you through three farm evaluations models that help you apply quantitative and qualitative analysis to your decision-making process.

Part 3 – How to Farm – This section provides a nuts and bolts description of what you need to begin farming and to sustain your farming for long term success.

Part 4 – Reviewing Your Farming Performance – Once you have some track record with your farm, this section provides a framework for evaluating and improving your farming performance.

Farming is something that takes great commitment over a long period of time. In other words, it's a journey of a thousand miles. My goal is that this book will provide you with the first step on that journey to a successful real estate career.

Part 1 – Prospecting for Business

"We are what we repeatedly do. Excellence, then, is not an act, but a habit."

— Aristotle

You've probably heard of the 80/20 rule. A common example would be that 20% of the activities you perform deliver 80% of the results. In real estate, the most important example of the 80/20 rule is that 20% of the agents transact 80% of the business with predictable regularity.

In order to be a successful real estate agent and put yourself on the right side of the 80/20 rule, you need to develop a consistent source of business. While each agent will develop his or her own unique approach, there are several identifiable prospecting methods that can be used to develop a consistent source of business. This section provides a high-level overview of these various methods.

Chapter 1 – Prospecting Methods

While this section identifies different prospecting channels that have proven to be effective for real estate agents, it is important to point out that most agents apply more than one prospecting channel to their business. However, when a particular channel proves to be more effective than others, agents tend to place more emphasis on that particular channel.

Referrals
Referrals are a great channel of business and many real estate agents are able to thrive working purely on referrals. When you start in the business, your friends, family and former colleagues form what is called your Sphere of Influence. This is the group of people with whom you've developed relationships over the years. These are also the people who most want to see you succeed in the business. As such, you should actively and regularly ask for referrals from your Sphere of Influence. Over time, former clients will be added and your Sphere of Influence will grow. Always remember to communicate regularly with your Sphere of Influence as this is your best source of referrals.

Open House
Another channel is to hold an open house for another agent. Listing agents are often too busy or have too many listings to be able to hold all of their listings open. Many agents have built their businesses by hosting open houses for other agents. While there are many curiosity-seekers at open houses, potential buyers visit open houses in the neighborhoods in which they are interested. Neighbors from the surrounding area also frequent open houses, often because they are considering selling themselves and are trying to get a feel for the value of their own home.

The downside of an open house is that you have almost no control over who will show up, and unless you have your own listings to hold open, you rely on other agents for prospecting.

Cancelled and Expired Listings

Another recurring source of business is to monitor the Cancelled and Expired listings in your area. You can easily set up a daily search online and follow up with these potential sellers by mail, phone or by knocking on their door. Be certain that the listing is actually cancelled or expired before contacting the seller to steer clear of any problems with the previous listing agent.

For Sale By Owner

Similarly, many agents have found success in converting For Sale By Owner (FSBO) sellers into listing clients. Research shows that approximately 60% of sellers who attempt to sell their home themselves ultimately list their home for sale with a real estate agent. To identify these potential clients, scan the newspaper, search websites like Craigslist® that FSBOs use and look for For Sale By Owner signs in your coverage area.

Door Knocking

Door knocking is most appropriate when you are working in a geographic farm, or when you have a listing. If you have a listing, you can knock on doors in the neighborhood to invite neighbors (i.e., potential sellers) to your open house. This gives you the opportunity to create a personal connection with potential sellers and to ask for referrals in the neighborhood. You can ask them if they know of anyone looking to move into the neighborhood. A report highlighting local market activity in the neighborhood is probably the information most valued by homeowners and is a great leave-behind when door knocking.

Cold Calling

Calling people you don't know and asking for their business is probably the most challenging method of prospecting. Many consumers find the practice to be invasive, and that is why the

Do Not Call Registry was created. However, successful sales professionals are successful because they do things their less successful colleagues are unwilling to do. Cold calling, like most prospecting methods, is a numbers game. In other words, you may have to go through a hundred "No's" before you get to your first "Yes." If you decide to cold call, make sure your call list is scrubbed against the Do Not Call list to avoid incurring costly fines.

Floor Time

There was a time when the only way to find out about a listing was to call or visit a real estate office to inquire about a listing. Today, virtually everything there is to know about a listing is available online. As such, the value of floor time has diminished over the years. However, in certain circumstances (like in the middle of a major city or in a vacation destination), floor time may still produce qualified leads from foot traffic and sign calls.

Online Prospecting

A more recent method of creating a channel is to advertise or participate in various online promotional opportunities. There are dozens of different business models in the online realm in which real estate agents can participate. One common method is to advertise using Pay per Click ads.

Pay per Click ads are displayed on search engines when someone types in a search term. For example, if you are targeting Beverly Hills, you might create a pay per click ad that offers a market report for Beverly Hills. When someone types Beverly Hills into the search engine and clicks on your ad, you pay the search engine for that click (hence, pay per click).

Typically, you set a budget for your ad and when you've reached your budgetary limit, your ad no longer appears. This has the benefit of being highly targeted, and it also enables you to set a budget that you will not exceed. Over time, you have the opportunity to build a reputation in a certain area (e.g., Beverly Hills) or practice type (e.g., working with seniors).

You can also advertise on an ever-growing list of websites devoted to some aspect of real estate. The best of these enable you to target the area where your ad will appear. Much like a general search engine, many of these sites have property search engines or provide market data by geographic area. You can buy ad space on search sites like Trulia® in the areas where you hope to build your business.

Another method of creating a channel is to participate in online forums where buyers, sellers and agents interact. For example, many real estate websites give visitors the opportunity to post questions to that online community. Agents who participate can answer these questions and build rapport with potential clients.

Social Media
Social media sites like Twitter®, Facebook® and LinkedIn® offer outstanding tools to create close relationships with your Sphere of Influence. If you are able to connect with your friends, family and clients using social media, you can interact with them on a regular and cost-effective basis.

You can also use these tools to post content (e.g., images, community information, statistics, etc.) about your coverage area to build relationships in your target areas. You can also use these tools to promote your listings and sales to demonstrate your proof of production.

Become a Buyer's Agent
Many top producing listing agents decide that it is better for them to work with a designated buyer's agent than to deal with buyers themselves. Listing agents tend to generate numerous buyer leads and their buyer's agent can focus on serving those

clients. Usually, the listing agent gets a referral fee (e.g., 25% of the buyer's side of the commission) on all closed transactions. However, the arrangement between agents is subject to personal relationships and negotiation.

The benefit to being a buyer's agent is that you get a consistent source of buyer leads. The benefit to the listing agent is that they are able to make a commission on the referred buyer leads, and they can potentially sell the homes of those referred buyers when the time comes to sell their house.

Farming
Finally, there is the prospecting method that I think works best and to which the rest of this book is dedicated. When I first entered the business, I quickly realized that the top producers in my office had developed a consistent source of business from farms they had been cultivating for years. I was amazed how these agents had new listings, week in and week out.

From the outside looking in, it appeared that all they did was answer the phone and take orders for new listings. I knew it wasn't that easy, but I immediately decided that I wanted to emulate those top-producing agents. Within weeks of starting in the business, I created a plan to start farming.

Like most agents, I went through a period of trial and error where I tried to re-invent the wheel. I learned from my mistakes and continued to refine my approach. Ultimately, I developed a system that took the proven techniques used by others and added some of the principles of marketing communications that I had learned in business school. That system enabled me to achieve success through farming very quickly.

By my third year in the business, I had achieved the International President's Circle award-level at Coldwell Banker®. When I would get a new listing in my farm, other agents would ask me details on how I got the listing, how long I had been farming, what kind of marketing I did in my farm, etc.

Many told me they had farmed in the past without success. It soon became clear to me that while a lot of agents wanted to be successful farmers, most of these agents did not have a coherent farming plan. That gap in knowledge motivated me to write this book so that any agent could acquire the fundamental skills needed to be a successful farmer.

Chapter 2 – What is Farming?

Why do they call it farming? In sales, we speak of hunters and farmers. Hunters are generally the rare breed that can penetrate and land a new account for themselves or their company. A farmer is usually a person assigned to an account to manage the relationship and to maximize the revenue from the account.

In real estate, a farmer is an individual or team that manages an "account" to maximize sales. While there are other audiences you can farm, in most cases, the account is a neighborhood or area of a city that the farmer intends to service. Think of an actual farmer, one who grows crops for food production, to better understand real estate farming.

A farmer works a tract of land and his job is to make the most productive use of that land. The farmer must carefully evaluate his farm and determine the types of crops that will prosper in the topography and climate where his farm is located.

His goal is to maximize his earnings from the farm. If he chooses a crop that is ill suited to that location, he will lose a lot of money and waste a lot of time. He may not make it to the next planting season.

The farmer must make a plan for the entire year, not just the harvest season. He then has to work that plan diligently throughout the year by getting up early and working late. He must plant seeds at the right time to make sure that his crop will prosper when the weather conditions are best to grow his crop. He needs to be ready to harvest his crop when it is mature, and work overtime to make sure the opportunity does not pass him by.

After he's harvested his crop, he must plow under the remains to nurture the soil for the next planting season. Furthermore, he must rotate his crops to make sure that he does not exhaust his soil.

Our hard-working farmer must also monitor local, state and federal government agencies to determine how their actions will affect his ability to run his farm profitably. He must hope that weather conditions don't ruin his crops. Lastly, he must be an expert in running his farm, but he must also manage his farm like a business, making sure to re-invest in the business so that he can sustain himself over the long haul.

As a real estate agent who farms, you must be as productive and multi-talented as our friend, the hard-working farmer. Like the farmer, you must assess your prospective farm and make sure that the conditions are right for successful farming. A neighborhood in which only one or two homes sell each year is not a very productive farm.

Like the farmer, you must plan for the entire year, not just the spring selling season. Many agents get caught up in the day-to-day minutiae of the business, or they get busy with a few clients and they stop prospecting.

Likewise, if you stop prospecting, your business will wither as though it was hit by drought or a plague. Like the farmer, you need to have a plan for the entire year, and then work that plan throughout the year. Just as the farmer plants seeds, you need to market yourself consistently, with the right message at the right time, to ensure that you'll get your fair share of business.

When it comes time to harvest your efforts, you need to be able to keep up with the increased workload associated with working more transactions. Traditionally, farmers worked in the light of the harvest moon to extend their workday during harvest season. You'll also be working long hours when you get more transactions from your farming efforts.

When a transaction is closed, and your current clients become past clients, you need to plow them back into your farm so they can enrich your business with referrals. Never make the mistake of letting past clients fall out of touch, because there will always be another agent happy to take their business and referrals.

Just as the former rotates his crops to keep his yields high, you'll need to make sure your marketing does not get stale and negatively impact your business. Review your marketing plan at least annually to make sure it's still on target. Also, remember to invest in training and continuing education so that you're always growing as an agent and a farmer.

You too must monitor local, state and federal agencies to understand how their actions will impact your business. From local signage ordinances to federal conforming loan limits, government agencies have a significant influence on your ability to make a living as a real estate agent. Your affiliation with REALTOR® organizations is your best bet for making sure your voice is heard by governmental agencies.

Weather conditions can have a big impact on a farmer. A bad freeze can wipe out a citrus crop in less than a week. Similarly, market conditions can greatly affect a real estate agent. It is your job to monitor market conditions and take pro-active steps to adapt to these dynamic economic forces. For example, if financing and underwriting guidelines change dramatically, you need to adapt to make sure you are able to serve your clients effectively.

Finally, you must run your real estate practice like a business. You need to establish goals and objectives that you want to achieve. You must then create a plan that will help you achieve those objectives. We're not talking about changing your attitude so you can be successful. We're talking about identifying concrete steps that you must take to achieve your goals.

This will start with a high-level objective like closing 20 sales during the year, and it will translate into a specific work plan that might include direct mail and sponsoring a zip code in your farm on a major real estate search site like Trulia®.

You must then allocate the time and financial resources you'll need to achieve those objectives. Many agents think they can create a successful real estate practice without spending very much money on marketing. If you're serious about your real estate practice, you need to think in terms of spending five to ten percent of your projected gross commission income on your marketing plan. This book will help you develop your business objectives and the marketing plan those objectives imply.

FARMING DEFINED
In the past, farming usually meant sending direct mail to a geographic neighborhood. I like to broaden the definition of farming to include all the varied activities described in this book, and to include any audience one decides to target with their farming.

My definition of farming is as follows: "*Farming is the process of marketing consistently to a well-defined target audience to generate leads, repeat business and referrals.*" As this definition indicates, the whole point of prospecting is to generate leads. The progression of a lead is shown in Figure 1.

Figure 1 – Progression of a Lead
Suspect → Prospect → Unqualified Lead → Qualified Lead → Client

Moving from left to right, a suspect is someone in who is a member of your target audience. You suspect that they may be a candidate to one day be your customer. A prospect is someone you've had some form of contact with. They may have received a post card from you, or maybe visited your website. An unqualified lead is someone that you establish a connection with, but you know little or nothing about his or her situation or motivation level.

A qualified lead is someone with whom you've engaged in conversation, and with whom you have at least a basic understanding of his or he situation and motivation level. Finally, a client is someone you have converted to work with you.

Once you have converted a suspect into a client, you need to continue your prospecting efforts. When someone hires you to list their home, or assist them in buying a home, there are several truisms that come into play that can help you in your prospecting:

- *Your new client is likely to have a favorable opinion of you.* Take advantage of this honeymoon period to garner referrals from your new client. Don't be afraid to ask questions like, "So, do you have any friends or family members who are thinking about getting into the market?"

- *The transaction is very likely the focal point of their lives.* You will be amazed by how consumed a buyer or seller can be when they're living through the process. You'll be equally amazed by how quickly they will get out of that mode once the transaction is completed. Clients who can't remember the name of the agent who helped them buy or sell a home previously have shocked me. As real estate practitioners, we're in the market every day. We forget how all consuming and emotional it can be for our clients who are involved only sporadically. There is no time like the present when it comes to asking for referrals from new clients.

- ***Clients who are in the market are attuned to others in similar situations***. When you're thinking about buying a certain kind of car, you seem to see that car wherever you drive. There is a heightened sense of awareness that comes when we are in the market for those types of big-ticket items. When someone is in the real estate market (buyers or sellers), they have a heightened awareness of others that are looking, thinking of selling or already on the market. This is especially true given the prevalence of social media. Don't assume that their friends or family members have representation or that they are satisfied with their current representation. A little probing will let you know whether or not there is an opportunity for you to gain additional clients.

You worked hard to get your new client. Your goal should be to secure one to three qualified leads from each of your clients. Of course, each client goes into your sphere of influence so that you maintain a lifelong relationship that will generate repeat business and ongoing referrals. Failure to cultivate your sphere of influence is usually fatal to a real estate career.

Chapter 3 – Types of Farms

The traditional view of farming is that it involves a geographic farm. In other words, a farm that is defined by geographical boundaries like streets, creeks, schools, etc. However, there are many different types of target audiences to which you can apply my definition of farming. This section will identify the different types of target audiences you might consider farming.

Geographic
Geographic farms remain the most common type of farm. This makes sense because local market knowledge is so critical in real estate sales. If you've been in real estate for any length of time, you know of at least a few successful geographic farmers. In other words, agents who "own" a certain area. How they began to farm that area varies by agent. For some, the decision involved laborious analysis. For others, it may be as simple as something like, "Well, I got a listing in that area, and one thing led to another..."

While some have criticized geographic farming as antiquated as more buyers and sellers move online, I firmly believe that geographic farming will be a viable business model for the foreseeable future. Real estate is ultimately a relationship business, and geographic farming gives you a proven vehicle in which to cultivate long-term relationships with your target audience. A geographic farm is usually defined by one or more clearly identifiable geographic traits:

- Subdivision or distinct neighborhood
- Condo or townhouse community
- School attendance area
- City boundaries
- Near downtown areas
- Any other geographic trait that defines an area

An example description of a geographic farm might be as follows: *"Homes in the city of Bedford belonging to the Creekside School District, bounded by Sax Street on the north, Mills Parkway on the west, the Chester County Expressway on the east and Mills River on the south."* Being able to delineate your farm with this much precision will greatly assist in the development of your marketing program.

Sphere of Influence

The second most common type of farm is a Sphere of Influence farm. Your Sphere of Influence, often referred to simply as your sphere, consists of all the people you know who are either prospects, referral sources or both.

This includes your family, friends, neighbors, past clients, former co-workers, acquaintances from church, parents at your child's school, your hair stylist, your dentist, your doctor, the owner of the bagel shop, etc. Anyone you know who is in even the slightest position to hire you or refer someone to you is in your sphere.

How do you manager your sphere? First and foremost is to let them know you're in the business! You can do this in conversations, via email, social media and direct mail. The most important thing is to stay in regular communication with your sphere, and to ask for referrals forthrightly and unapologetically. You can't grow your real estate practice if you're too timid to ask for more business.

Whether you've been in the business for decades or days, the most important thing you can do for your business is to set up a contact management database populated by people in your sphere. This database should include the following required information (you can assemble the nice-to-have information over time, don't get stuck just because you don't have all the nice-to-haves):

<u>Required</u>
- Name
- Spouse's Name (if applicable)
- Address
- Phone Number
- How you know them (Neighbor, Family, Church, etc.)

<u>Nice-to-Have</u>
- Names of Kids (if applicable)
- Birthdays for everyone in the immediate family
- Email Address
- Employer
- Job Title
- If a past client, notes on their transaction(s)
- Notes about the person (likes, dislikes)
- Notes regarding conversations you've had with the contact

You'll use this information to stay in contact with those in your sphere and to reference when you interact with them. For example, you should send birthday cards to everyone in your sphere. You'd be a superstar if you send them to their kids also. Your sphere database is your most important asset. Make sure you devote the necessary time to create and maintain it.

Absentee Owners
These are property owners who rent their property to tenants, and are thus "absent." Landlords and investors tend to look at property ownership differently than standard homeowners. Standard homeowners tend to associate themselves with a home and thus have an emotional connection to the home. Landlords see property as an asset, something to be managed and maintained, that generates cash flow and, hopefully, appreciates in value over the long haul. Farming to absentee owners involves a completely different type of message than you would employ in a standard geographic farm.

For example, sending a "Local Events" post card to a geographic farm may make sense, but an absentee owner living in a different city would probably find this to be of little value. Messaging that focuses on the investment aspects of property ownership would be much more relevant.

Identifying absentee owners is a relatively straightforward exercise. When searching mailing lists, look for homes that have a different mailing address than the site address. This is an indication that the owner does not live at the property. In other words, he or she is an absentee owner. You may find absentee owners in bunches (i.e., a pocket of duplexes near your home), or you may find them distributed throughout an entire city or even a county.

Renters
While we tend to think of farming as something targeting only homeowners, it may make sense to farm renters who may become homeowners. A perfect example might be an apartment complex where the rents are roughly comparable to what it would cost to buy an entry-level home in the same area. You could target these homeowners and help them buy their first home.

As noted earlier, one of the goals of working with buyers is the fact that you might be called on to sell their home when the time comes. This makes it easier for you on two levels. First, you already have a relationship with the seller. Second, you already know the house well because you helped the seller buy the home in the first place.

Affinity
An affinity group is simply a group to which you belong that shares a common interest or trait. A good example of an affinity group is an alumni organization of a high school or university. Typically, organizations or associations are formed for affinity groups that you can join.

A chamber of commerce would be another type of affinity group. Because you share a connection with others in an affinity group, you can leverage that mutual trait or interest to create contacts that you can farm.

As you can see, there are many different types of farms. You might even be able to think of additional types of farms. However, the only thing more important than identifying the type of farm you want to target is to prospect consistently into that farm once you've identified your target farm(s).

Profile: The Successful Farmer
To illustrate what it means to be a successful farmer, consider the case of a real estate professional I met when I started in the business. He is well liked by his colleagues, cooperating brokers and his managing broker. He sells approximately 40 homes a year, year in and year out. He has an assistant who handles most of the administrative workload, and a buyer's agent to handle buyers.

This successful farmer has built his farm by employing a combination of direct mail, print ads and hosting open houses in his farms. He is sure to host the first open house to increase the likelihood of meeting neighbors who tend to visit open houses early in the process. He also lives near the neighborhood, so homeowners see him around town in the local shops and restaurants.

He also sends a calendar to his farm every year and neighbors have come to expect their annual delivery. This calendar keeps his image and contact information visible to his prospects throughout the year. He supports local charities by asking homeowners in his farm to nominate organizations who are making a difference in their local community.

The farm itself consists of moderately priced homes that are in a classic "build equity and then move-up" neighborhood. This ensures predictable turnover in the neighborhood.

This real estate professional has been farming the area for so long that virtually every homeowner in the neighborhood knows who this farmer is and that he sells the most homes in their neighborhood. The strength of this agent's brand in the market enables him to take several meaningful vacations every year to spend time with his wife and family.

In short, this agent has built the type of real estate practice that any real estate professional would love to have. The good news is that this type of success can be emulated. That is the purpose of this book – to give you a blue print to follow to start and manage a farm for long-term success.

Part 2 – The Farm Evaluation Process

"Far and away the best prize that life has to offer is the chance to work hard at work worth doing."

—— Theodore Roosevelt

This part of the book is designed to help you determine whether you are suited to farming, and if you are, how to evaluate the farms you are considering. I will walk you through three farm evaluation frameworks you can use to help determine whether the farms you are considering make good business sense. While these frameworks are useful tools, you should discuss your findings with your manager, broker or mentor to get their perspective on whether you're taking the correct course of action.

Chapter 4 – Self-Analysis

The first step in the farm evaluation process is some basic self-analysis to determine if you are suited to farming. As you answer the following questions, be honest with yourself. If you think you are giving the "right" answer and it's not a true reflection of your nature, you're just deluding yourself and wasting your time. One of the main reasons for this book is to help you determine if farming is the right prospecting channel for you. So, take a moment to think about and answer the following questions:

1. In general, I am:
    a. Process-oriented (Same tasks done again and again)
    b. Project-oriented (Different tasks with definite end dates)

2. In my work life, I tend to:
    a. Figure out what works best and then stick with it
    b. Try lots of different things and test the different outcomes

3. In my work life, if I have to do the same things over and over:
    a. I get comfortable with the routine
    b. I get bored with the routine

4. In my career, I have tended to:
    a. Stay with the same companies for long periods of time
    b. Move around a lot to different companies

5. I am happiest with:
    a. The comfort of knowing what to expect
    b. The excitement of discovering something new

If you finished most of the sentences above with an "a" you are more likely to have the mindset of a farmer. If you finished most of the sentences above with a "b" you are likely not to be pre-disposed to be a farming candidate.

While this exercise points to extremes in behavior types, you should be aware that farming is a long-term prospecting method in which you perform some fairly repetitive tasks. While this can lead to a predictable source of income, there are some real estate professionals whose personality does not fit the behavioral mindset that is required to be successful.

Think of the difference between a farmer and a hunter. A farmer performs the same set of tasks every season, year in and year out. It's not exciting, but he can count on a predictable harvest as long as external conditions like the weather don't wipe him out.

A hunter, by contrast, has the proverbial thrill of the hunt. He's out in the forest, seeing new things, smelling new smells and tasting new tastes. He relishes the freedom that comes from being able to follow any trail that looks promising. He may catch his prey, he may not. If he does catch his prey, he may reap a huge bounty. Then again, he may starve. That's all part of the excitement.

If you finished most sentences above with a "b," don't despair; there are many prospecting methods that fit your personality that will enable you to be successful in real estate. You should identify ways that you can channel your project-oriented nature to meet new people and explore different ways of connecting with people. You'll also be most likely to identify and exploit new methods of prospecting as they emerge. You are a hunter, and you should go forth, unapologetically, into the fray.

Chapter 5 – Why You Need to Evaluate Farms

If you decide you are a farming candidate, you need to move on to the next step in the evaluation process. I have developed three farm evaluation frameworks to assist you in your analysis. Take your time in this phase; because once you have started farming, the financial cost and opportunity cost of abandoning a farm can be painful, and possibly fatal to your real estate career.

When I first started farming, I did a very cursory analysis of the area I chose. I selected it primarily because the price points were in the mid-range of the market and I was familiar with the area having grown up nearby. What I did not realize until I had farmed the area for some time was that the people who lived in that farm were the type of people who tended not to hire agents from full-service brokerages like mine. Had I done more analysis, I would have realized that not only was there a dominant farmer in the area, but that most of the listings in the area were held by discount brokerages.

My type of full-service offering was out of step with that market. When I finally landed my first listing in that farm, I did the job for half my normal commission as I was competing with discounters, but also because I was desperate to get a listing in my farm. My goal was to leverage that first listing into many more, but it turned out to be my last in that area.

When I finally decided to abandon my original farm, I had sunk a significant amount of money into the farm that would do me no good in the future. More importantly, I had spent a year of my career spinning my wheels when I could have been cultivating another farm that would be a better fit (in other words, a huge opportunity cost).

The following sections describe the three farm evaluation models I have created to help you evaluate potential farms:

1. The 2x2 Farming Framework
2. The 10x10 Farm Evaluation Survey
3. The Farm Revenue Forecast

When you have performed the analysis for all of these methods, you will have a much clearer idea of where and/or whom to farm. While these frameworks are most applicable to geographic farms, the concepts can also be applied to other farm types.

Chapter 6 – The 2x2 Farming Framework

The first farm evaluation method is the 2x2 Farming Framework. Without question, the two most important elements that affect the viability of a farm are the price points and the level of turnover in the farm. If you are evaluating a geographic farm, you can use online sources to analyze the sales and pricing trends in the farm.

You should review at least three years of sales data for this step. Look at absolute prices and look at the trends in these prices.

Are prices increasing or decreasing dramatically? What is causing this trend? Are big changes affecting prices (e.g., school district changing school boundaries), or are temporary market conditions affecting prices? Are prices stable? If so, what is causing prices to be stable in this community? In other words, you need to have a deep understanding of the forces that affect prices, not just the absolute numbers.

Figure 2: The 2x2 Farming Framework

	Low Turnover	High Turnover
High Prices	PIG	COW
Low Prices	DOG	CHICKEN

Next, look at the turnover in the farm. You calculate turnover by dividing the number of sales over the course of a year by the total number of homes in the farm. For example, assume you are reviewing a farm that has 1,000 homes.

The number of sales in this farm over the last three years was 70, 50 and 60. To calculate turnover rate, take the number of sales and divide by the total number of homes. For year one, turnover is 70 divided by 1,000 for a turnover rate of 7%.

Calculate the next two years and you have turnover rates of 7%, 5% and 6% for the last three years, or an average of 6%. Seven percent is considered the gold standard for farm turnover, so the farm in this example is just slightly below the ideal. However, it is still well worth further consideration.

Pricing and turnover are two critical factors that impact the viability of a farm. Looking at them together will help you decide whether it is the right farm for you. To illustrate how these concepts work together, I have developed a Farming Framework based on the concept of a 2x2 matrix. The way a 2x2 matrix works is that you have an X-axis with a certain characteristic, and a Y-axis with another characteristic.

In the Farming Framework, the X-axis (horizontal) characteristic is Turnover, and the Y-axis (vertical) characteristic is Pricing. You then look at one of the four boxes created in the 2x2 matrix. For example, a farm with low prices and low turnover (bottom left quadrant) would be characterized as a Dog in the Farming Framework.

Let's look more closely at each type of farm. Think of the different types of farms in the 2x2 Farming Framework as different types of animals, and think about how effective they would be in terms of feeding you and your family.

COW

This type of farm is the holy grail of all farms. You have high prices and high turnover. This farm is as productive as a cow. A cow gives you milk which can use to drink or to make into cheese, yogurt, cream, cottage cheese, ice cream, etc. It can also give you juicy steaks, and lots of them.

A cow market might be found in an urban market where the prices are high and there is a steady turnover of housing stock. The only problem with cow farms is that they attract a lot of farmers. If the farm exhibits cow traits, try to determine how much competition there is in the farm.

PIG

A pig is an interesting creature that can even give you companionship as it matures. Unfortunately for your family, it does not provide any food as it is growing to maturity. However, it ultimately provides a bounty of delicious meats including bacon, pork chops and pork loin. A pig could feed not just your family, but also an entire Hawaiian luau.

A Pig farm is usually an affluent farm in which there is low turnover. The people who live in these types of neighborhoods have already arrived, so they're not the type of homeowners who are still looking to trade up. Moves in these types of farms are generated mostly by lifestyle-related factors like job transfers, divorces, retirement, etc.

While the quantity of sales in a pig farm is less than you'd like to see, this is at least partially offset by the higher commission you'll receive on each sale due to the higher pricing. Be careful with these types of farms, however. Many agents like to farm affluent areas because they feel the neighborhood is a reflection of their status as an agent.

CHICKEN

A chicken is a wondrous animal that can give you both eggs and, eventually, a little bit of meat. You can't feed an entire Luau with a chicken, but it can feed your family for a night. A chicken farm is one in which the prices are low, but there is a lot of turnover because homeowners are regularly looking to trade up. The classic example would be a starter home like a condo or small house that the homeowner eventually outgrows. While you make less per transaction, you make it up on volume in a chicken farm.

DOG

A dog can be a fantastic companion, but it's going to do little to help feed your family. A dog farm is a farm that not only has low prices, but there is also little turnover. Usually, these are depressed neighborhoods where there is limited appreciation, and limited demand. Homeowners move in based on getting a good value, and they tend to stay because they don't build up the equity they need to move up. As the name implies, you should avoid a dog farm as it will consume your resources and give you no food in return.

Performing this exercise can be very informative, and it gives you some thoughts on how to evaluate potential farms using two of the most important quantitative measures of farm productivity. Subjective factors like whether you live in your farm will be discussed later on. Let's look at some examples to further illustrate how to use this framework.

Chapter 7 – Using the 2x2 Farming Framework

This chapter demonstrates how you might use the 2x2 Farming Framework using some hypothetical examples.

HANOVER HEIGHTS
Built less than 5 years ago, Hanover Heights is a master-planned community designed around three championship-level golf courses, a country club, an upscale fitness center and a full-service spa. All of the homes in Hanover Heights are larger than the average home in the area, and each has an amazing view of the golf courses and/or the surrounding mountains.

The homes are designed to be executive homes with high-end telecommunications and home entertainment features like whole house audio built into the homes. Each of the homes has a large office on the ground floor.

The people who live in Hanover Heights are typically managers at one of the numerous biotech companies that are concentrated in this area. It's a beautifully maintained neighborhood, and it is well known by relocation specialists who support the local biotech companies. There is another area of the country that has a high concentration of biotech companies. In most cases, companies have operations in both locations.

As such, there is a lot of moving back and forth between these two biotech centers as employees get transferred or change jobs. There are 358 homes in Hanover Heights. The median price in the city where Hanover Heights is located hovers around $500,000 and it has been fairly stable over the last three years.

Let's look at the Farming Framework numbers for the last three years at Hanover Heights:

YEAR	MEDIAN PRICES	TURNOVER
1	$658,000	8%
2	$669,000	10%
3	$679,000	7%
Average	**$668,000**	**8.3%**

Hanover Heights has a median price that is quite a bit higher than the median prices in the city. The average median price over the last three years was approximately $668,000, or $168,000 over the city median of $500,000. Moreover, homes are appreciating while the city median has remained flat for the last three years. We can conclude that on a relative basis, Hanover Heights has higher prices than other parts of the city we may be evaluating.

First, we evaluate Hanover Heights using the Farming Framework. The average median price of the homes in Hanover Heights is higher than the rest of the city. Moreover, pricing is trending up in this sub-division even as the city's prices remain flat. This information would lead one to put Hanover Heights in the "High Prices" category.

The next step in evaluating the potential farm is to look at turnover rates. Turnover has averaged 8.3% over the last three years. The benchmark I use when evaluating turnover is whether the turnover rate is less than or greater than 7%. Farms with turnover rates less than 7% would be considered "Low Turnover" while those with rates higher than 7% would be considered "High Turnover." Hanover Heights' turnover rate is 8.3% making it a High Turnover farm.

Combining the two metrics, we see that Hanover Heights is a "High Prices" and "High Turnover" potential farm. This classifies it as a "Cow" farm. As noted earlier, this is the best possible type of farm, if you ignore competition level. Considering that Hanover Heights is probably the most prestigious area of the city, you can safely predict that there are many agents interested in the farm for both its Cow attributes and also the prestige-factor that goes along with farming the area.

SERENE MEADOWS

One of the original areas to be developed in the area, Serene Meadows was literally a quiet meadow before being built-out as a housing sub-division. The homes were built shortly after World War II, when building materials were still scarce. As such, the homes in this sub-division were quite modest. All of the homes were built as three bedrooms and one bathroom, the norm for that time period, with between 1,000 to 1,200 square feet of living space depending on the floor plan. Each home had a two-car garage, a novelty at the time. There were four floor plans that were alternated along the street with the pattern repeating throughout the subdivision.

The homes were initially built to house the many former service men and engineers and their families who moved to the area to work in the nascent aerospace industry in the region. In the initial Serene Meadows sub-division, there were a total of 346 homes. Subsequent developments in the immediate surrounding area followed the general style and configurations of the original sub-division and brought the total number of homes in the greater neighborhood to 508.

During the 1950's and 1960's, Serene Meadows was the profile of post-war, middle-class suburban living. The region's first shopping mall opened in the neighborhood in 1958. Schools were full of baby boom kids, and the neighborhood was considered desirable.

Over time, additional sub-divisions were built in the areas surrounding the original section of town. Homes in the newer sub-divisions were larger and more modern. Families began to trade up out of Serene Meadows for these newer sub-divisions. As time passed, some of the homes in the area began to fall into disrepair. In the 1970's one of the two elementary schools in the neighborhood was closed due to declining enrollment and budget cuts.

By the 1980's, more and more homes began to fall into disrepair. The mall that had been a source of pride for so long was 30% vacant by the early 1990's. It went through several remodels hoping to re-capture its earlier glory days, but nothing seemed to work. By the late 1990's, more than 40% of residents were renters. The home values in Serene Meadows had not kept pace with the rest of the city and the median price of the homes was now far below the city average.

Serene Meadows became a neighborhood where first-time homebuyers bought homes in order to own their own home for roughly the cost of renting in more desirable neighborhoods. Primarily a blue collar and service industry neighborhood, Serene Meadows residents tended to live in their homes for a long time, mostly because they did not have sufficient equity to trade up to better neighborhoods.

However, many of the residents enjoyed the character of their neighborhood, in addition to the strong social fabric they enjoyed with other long-time neighbors living in the sub-division. Some of the homeowners began to show pride of ownership in their homes, with modest remodeling and landscaping projects becoming more commonplace.

Let's look at the Farming Framework numbers for the last three years at Serene Meadows:

YEAR	MEDIAN PRICES	TURNOVER
1	$220,000	3.7%
2	$217,000	4.3%
3	$219,000	3.9%
Average	$218,667	3.9%

Serene Meadows has a median price that is quite a bit lower than the median prices in the city. The average median price over the last three years was approximately $218,000, or a whopping $209,000 less than the city median of $427,000. Moreover, home prices have been flat over the last three years, while the city's median price has been rising for the last three straight years. We can conclude that on a relative basis, Serene Meadows has lower prices than other parts of the city we may be evaluating.

The first step in evaluating Serene Meadows using the 2x2 Farming Framework is to make a conclusion about pricing. The average median price of the homes in Serene Meadows is lower than the rest of the city. Moreover, pricing is flat in this sub-division even as the city's prices are appreciating. This information would lead one to put Serene Meadows in the "Low Prices" category.

The next step in evaluating the potential farm is to look at turnover rates. Turnover has averaged 3.9% over the last three years. The benchmark I use when evaluating turnover is whether the turnover rate is less than or greater than 7%. Farms with turnover rates less than 7% would be considered "Low Turnover" while those with rates higher than 7% would be considered "High Turnover." Serene Meadows' turnover rate is 3.9% making it a Low Turnover farm.

Combining the two metrics, we see that Serene Meadows is a "Low Prices" and "Low Turnover" potential farm. This classifies it as a "Dog" farm. As noted earlier, this is the worst possible type of farm, if you ignore competition level. Considering that Serene Meadows is probably the least desirable area of the city for real estate practitioners, you very well may be able to make it a workable farm, depending on your individual circumstances.

Even at a low turnover rate of 3.9%, that means that there are still 20 homes being sold there each year on average (508 total homes x 3.9% = 20 homes). An agent that dominates the farm could have a decent number of listings each year. However, the low price point on these sales likely makes the effort unjustified, because even the most dominant farmers rarely capture more than 20% market share in their farm. All things being equal, you should probably cross Serene Meadows off your list of potential farms.

HIDDEN OAKS

The Hidden Oaks neighborhood is home to both long-term residents and up-and-coming professionals who work in a variety of local companies. The city where Hidden Oaks is located is a bedroom community of a large city across the river that is home to many major players in the insurance industry. The area also boasts three world-class universities, and a busy port that is the focal point of a thriving seaboard. Companies choose to have their headquarters in this area because the business climate is friendly, and there is a steady source of skilled workers.

Hidden Oaks grew in concentric circles around its original downtown core, a highly popular area that provides a definitive focal point for the community. It is also an area that has significant architectural value and charm. The downtown area has numerous events throughout the year including parades, art and wine festivals, community concerts and a weekly farmer's market in the summer.

There are several four star restaurants, and numerous boutiques. However, there are also many Mom and Pop businesses that provide the basics for many residents of Hidden Oaks. In fact, Hidden Oaks residents take pride in their support of local merchants.

In addition to the downtown area, there is also an upscale, modern mall that serves the greater area. There are also several Big Box stores that provide Hidden Oaks residents with goods and services that are generally not available in the downtown area. In short, Hidden Oaks is a well-served community.

The homes in Hidden Oaks are a mixture of older craftsman-style homes, ranch homes built in the 1950's and 1960's, newer homes built during a period of growth in the 1990's and a handful of mansions that were built in the 1920's.

Despite the varying housing stock, the community blends together fairly seamlessly from block to block. Most of the homes are well kept, including neatly manicured landscaping. The total number of single-family homes in Hidden Oaks is just over 2,800.

Given all of its positive attributes, most residents consider Hidden Oaks to be a garden spot that they would never consider leaving voluntarily. The vast majority of moves out of the area are due to job transfers and changes in lifestyle (divorce, deaths in the family, etc.).

However, the high cost of living does weigh on many families, and some eventually seek less expensive areas further away from the large city, or in nearby adjoining states.

Let's look at the Farming Framework numbers for the last three years at Hidden Oaks:

YEAR	MEDIAN PRICES	TURNOVER
1	$1,089,000	4.8%
2	$1,107,000	5.1%
3	$1,118,000	3.7%
Average	**$1,104,667**	**4.5%**

Hidden Oaks has a median price that is quite a bit higher than the median prices in the immediate area. The average median price over the last three years was approximately $1,104,000, or $247,000 more than the city median of $857,000. Home prices have been rising over the last three years, and the city's median price has been rising at roughly the same rate of growth for the last three straight years. We can conclude that on a relative basis, Hidden Oaks has higher prices than other parts of the city we may be evaluating.

The first step in evaluating Hidden Oaks using the 2x2 Farming Framework is to make a conclusion about pricing. The average median price of the homes in Hidden Oaks is higher than the rest of the city. The median prices in Hidden Oaks and the rest of the city are rising at about the same rate. This information would lead one to put Hidden Oaks in the "High Prices" category.

The next step in evaluating the potential farm is to look at turnover rates. Turnover has averaged 4.5% over the last three years. The benchmark I use when evaluating turnover is whether the turnover rate is less than or greater than 7%. Farms with turnover rates less than 7% would be considered "Low Turnover" while those with rates higher than 7% would be considered "High Turnover." Hidden Oaks' turnover rate is 4.5% making it a Low Turnover farm.

Combining the two metrics, we see that Hidden Oaks is a "High Prices" and "Low Turnover" potential farm. This classifies it as a "Pig" farm. As noted earlier, this type of farm does not yield as many sales, but the higher prices per transaction may justify the lower transaction volume.

Moreover, the long-term desirability of the area leads one to believe that the long-term demand for homes in this area will be consistent. Thus, selling listings in this area should not be problematic.

As with all farms that have any positive attributes, you need to be concerned about potential and existing competition. However, looking at the size of the area (more than 2,800 homes), there is probably room for several successful farmers. At a turnover rate of 4.5%, one can expect 126 homes to be sold in Hidden Oaks each year. As long as you're getting a fair share of the business, Hidden Oaks is definitely worth considering as a potential farm.

PARKSIDE VILLAS
This master-planned upscale townhouse community was recently built around a new 18 acre park, called Homestead Heritage Park. Constructed at a cost of $2.3 million, the new park features an artificial lake for boating in addition to tennis courts, soccer fields, softball and little league fields among other amenities.

The park also commemorates the original settlers who homesteaded the area in the eighteenth century. The park was a costly tradeoff for the developer who agreed to fund the park in exchange for approval of 927 townhouse units surrounding the park.

The developer also received approval to build a mixed-use retail-office-condo mini-downtown along a prime area of the newly created waterfront. This new project was expected to relieve the chronic shortage of office space in the area that had seen little growth during the previous two decades due to space limitations in the immediate area.

The number of new residents was also expected to create outstanding retail and restaurant opportunities that hoped to take advantage of the picturesque setting that was created.

The entire project was built on the site of a former air force base that was de-commissioned in the 1990's and subsequently sold to the developer. Despite initial opposition from slow-growth advocates in the area, the whole project was considered to be a success and was often cited as a model for development by smart-growth advocates.

The new condo units created affordable options for first-time homebuyers and young families. The office space was also quickly leased, and the shops and restaurants in the community were doing better than expected. Parkside Villas, the townhouse component of the project, was equally successful. The various` phases of the project sold well, and soon Parkside Villas had become a desirable option for young professionals in the area.

Parkside Villas is located a short drive up the freeway from Hidden Oaks, the community profiled earlier. Whereas Hidden Oaks is the more established community, Parkside Villas was quickly recognized as the ideal project for those young professionals and families that preferred to buy and build equity rather than rent in the major city across the river. They also appreciated the newness of the homes and the modern amenities included in the homes including stainless steel appliances, granite countertops, hardwood floors and central air conditioning.

Despite the attractiveness of the homes and the amenities at Homestead Heritage Park, there was still a strong desire among many of the residents of the area to move to more established communities like Hidden Oaks.

This desire was fueled by a combination of social pressure to demonstrate upward mobility and a need for more space as families grew in size and age. In other words, many families found that they ultimately outgrew their beloved Parkside Villa townhouse. This meant that there was a healthy turnover of homes in the Parkside Villas subdivision.

Let's look at the Farming Framework numbers for the last three years at Parkside Villas:

YEAR	MEDIAN PRICES	TURNOVER
1	$689,000	8.7%
2	$694,000	9.3%
3	$703,000	9.5%
Average	$695,000	9.1%

Parkside Villas has a median price that is lower than the median prices in the immediate area. The average median price over the last three years was approximately $695,000, or $162,000 less than the city median of $857,000. Home prices have been rising over the last three years, and the city's median price has been rising at roughly the same rate of growth for the last three straight years. We can conclude that on a relative basis, Parkside Villas has lower prices than other parts of the city we may be evaluating.

The first step in evaluating Parkside Villas using the 2x2 Farming Framework is to make a conclusion about pricing. The average median price of the homes in Parkside Villas is lower than the rest of the city. The median prices in Parkside Villas and the rest of the city are rising at about the same rate. This information would lead one to put Parkside Villas in the "Low Prices" category.

The next step in evaluating the potential farm is to look at turnover rates. Turnover has averaged 9.1% over the last three years. The benchmark I use when evaluating turnover is whether the turnover rate is less than or greater than 7%. Farms with turnover rates less than 7% would be considered "Low Turnover" while those with rates higher than 7% would be considered "High Turnover." Parkside Villas' turnover rate is 9.1% making it a High Turnover farm.

Combining the two metrics, we see that Parkside Villas is a "Low Prices" and "High Turnover" potential farm. This classifies it as a "Chicken" farm. As noted earlier, this type of farm yields quite a few sales, but with a lower price per transaction.

Moreover, the long-term desirability of the area leads one to believe that the long-term demand for homes in this area will be consistent. Therefore, selling listings in this area should not be problematic. Parkside Villas appears to be a classic "Move-Up" farm, one on which a successful business can be established.

These examples give you a narrative that helps you understand how to use the Farming Framework. It is a worthwhile exercise to research your potential farm and write out the narrative for the farm. This will help you evaluate the farm based on the two most critical factors (price points and turnover).

Performing this writing exercise will give you a more intimate understanding of your farm, and it might even give you some text that you can incorporate into your marketing materials.

Chapter 8 – The 10x10 Farm Evaluation Survey

Once you've evaluated a potential farm using the 2x2 Farming Framework, you're ready to judge the quality of the farm using the 10x10 Farm Evaluation Survey (See Figure 3). I call it a 10x10 survey because there are ten questions and ten possible answers for each question.

Once you have completed the survey of the farm, you add up the total of the points you assigned for each question. You then review the 10x10 Farm Evaluations Survey Interpretative Scale (See Table 1) to help determine whether the farm is worth pursuing further.

As you complete survey, be as honest with yourself as possible. There is absolutely no point in trying to skew the numbers to make the farm look more favorable. If anything, you want to be as conservative as possible to make sure the farm is actually viable, and not a product of wishful thinking.

Figure 3 – The Farm Evaluation Survey

Instructions: Circle the number that is the most appropriate answer:

1. Is there a dominant farmer and/or Is the area heavily farmed?

Heavily Farmed						Not Heavily Farmed			
1	2	3	4	5	6	7	8	9	10

2. What is the average turnover for the past three years?

				As a Percentage					
1	2	3	4	5	6	7	8	9	10

3. Are the average prices above, below or about the same as the median for the county?

Below			About the Same						Above
1	2	3	4	5	6	7	8	9	10

4. How many homes are in the farm?

100	200	300	400	500	600	700	800	900	1000+
1	2	3	4	5	6	7	8	9	10

5. Where do you live relative to the farm?

> 5 miles			> 2.5 miles				Live in the Farm		
1	2	3	4	5	6	7	8	9	10

6. To what extent do you have social connections to those in the farm?

Few			Some					Numerous	
1	2	3	4	5	6	7	8	9	10

7. To what extent does the area have a cohesive neighborhood identity?

Little			Some					Strong	
1	2	3	4	5	6	7	8	9	10

8. To what extent can you identify groups of homeowners to tailor your message?

Little			Some					Strong	
1	2	3	4	5	6	7	8	9	10

9. How well do you know the area and how authoritatively can you discuss it?

Little Knowledge						Strong Knowledge			
1	2	3	4	5	6	7	8	9	10

10. How many homes have you sold in the farm already?

1	2	3	4	5	6	7	8	9	10

The concepts behind each of the questions in the survey are as follows:

1. **Dominant Farmer** – While it is certainly possible to penetrate a farm that is dominated by one or more farmers over a long period of time, it certainly does not make your job any easier. When someone is getting a much higher percentage of listings in a farm than anyone else, you're talking about someone with high name recognition, a strong brand and demonstrated proof of production. Overcoming these advantages will be an uphill battle, and you can rest assured that the farmer does not appreciate newcomers. Every situation is different and there are circumstances that can help you compete with a dominant farmer. Circumstances like: There's a dramatic demographic shift in the market that benefits you, your brokerage firm is making an aggressive push into a market, or simply the fact that the dominant farmer is approaching retirement. Circumstances like these can provide an opening that a newcomer might be able to exploit. In general, however, a dominant farmer is usually a negative for farm evaluation purposes.

2. **Turnover** – As discussed in the 2x2 Farming Framework section, turnover is a critical factor when evaluating a farm. You will need to calculate the turnover as defined in that earlier section. Once you have the turnover percentage, round the number down or up as needed and circle the answer that corresponds to your turnover percentage. In general, higher turnover is more favorable and lower turnover is less favorable. This is just like inventory turnover at retail establishment. Think of a clothing store. The more times the jeans turnover, the higher the revenue and profits will be for the year.

3. **Average Prices** – Like turnover, average pricing is a critical evaluation criterion for your potential farm. As discussed in the 2x2 Farming Framework section, average pricing affects your commission levels, so it is an important consideration for your farm. The 10x10 survey gives less weight to lower priced homes and greater weight to those with high prices for that very reason. As with all of the evaluation tools in this book, you need to keep in mind qualifying factors like the fact that higher priced homes may be more difficult to sell. All things being equal, though, you would rather sell homes that cost more because you'll net more in commissions.

4. **Farm Size** – On the whole, a bigger farm tends to be better than a smaller farm. While you can be successful in any size farm, there are certain advantages that come with a bigger farm. Assuming a normal turnover rate, a larger farm will produce more potential listings in a given year than a smaller farm. Also, if you start with a smaller farm, you invite more potential competition in adjacent areas. If you want to expand into those areas later, there might be an entrenched competitor. Finally, while it's hard to quantify, a certain level of critical mass seems to be necessary for a farm to be successful. This is partly due to economies of scale in fixed marketing expenses like print ads and signage. When you have a bigger farm, this type of fixed marketing will resonate with more people who are already familiar with you from your direct marketing and social interaction. While marketing to a bigger farm is more expensive as you're ramping up your farm, you will in all likelihood want to grow your farm as you gain experience in the business. Starting out with a bigger farm lays the foundation for your long-term success.

5. **Proximity to Farm** – Where you live relative to the farm is another critical aspect to your potential farming success. When you live in, or very close to, your farm, you benefit in

many ways. First, the people in your farm presumably know you from their personal interactions with you in the neighborhood, at the park, in the grocery store, etc. Second, you will always be able to make the case to sellers that no one knows the neighborhood better than you (and local knowledge is paramount when selling a home). Moreover, you can say that no one will be more motivated than you to get the highest possible price for their home because a higher price will directly benefit you if you are a homeowner. Finally, you will find it to be exceedingly convenient to manage client meetings, open houses and property showings if you live close to your listings. While you can be successful farming an area far from your home, there are some natural synergies that come with living in or close to your farm.

6. **Social Connections** – Marketing is the process of communicating your value proposition to your target market in a systematic fashion. You will employ a variety of marketing communications tools in your farming efforts. However, your personal interactions with people are how you begin to develop a professional and personal reputation. These social connections are also how you will begin to generate referrals and direct business with your sphere of influence in your farm. Therefore, the degree to which you have social connections with people in your farm is an important factor in evaluating a farm.

7. **Neighborhood Identity** – When a neighborhood has a strong identity, people within the community tend to take pride in their community. As you tailor your marketing materials to leverage that identity, your marketing will benefit from those positive connotations. In addition, as you market properties in the area, that strong identity will resonate with buyers who are familiar with the neighborhood's distinctiveness.

8. **Farm Knowledge** – There is no substitute for local market knowledge about a farm. There are at least three levels of knowledge that a good local agent would be familiar with.

   The first is product knowledge. The products in this case are the homes in the potential farm. Do you know what year they were built? Do you know who the builder was? Do you know the general property characteristics of the original homes (e.g., were they built with hardwood floors or wall to wall carpeting)? Can you speak authoritatively about the architectural style of the homes? Do you know roughly how many homes are in original condition and how many are remodeled? Do you know what the most common types of remodel projects are in the neighborhood? The more details you have about the homes in the area, the more perceived knowledge you will exhibit to potential clients in your farm.

   The next type of knowledge has to do with social forces that have affected the farm. Are you familiar with the general history of the neighborhood? What is the mix of long-time versus newer homeowners? Do you know how the demographics of the farm have changed over time? Do you know how attendance area policies have changed in the local school district? Do you know how the retail mix has evolved to become what it is today? Are you familiar with current initiatives under consideration by the city council that would affect the potential farm? The more knowledge you have regarding the area, the more confidently you can speak with potential clients.

   The final type of knowledge you will need is an understanding of the market forces at work in the potential farm. Do you know how many homes have sold in the farm over the last year. Do you know the average days on market for these homes? Are homes selling with multiple offers? Are most of the homes selling below, at or over the list price? Is the market heating up, cooling off or holding steady? Do you talk with other agents in the market on a daily basis to gauge the condition of the market?

In other words, do you know all there is to know about what's going on in the local real estate market? If you have your finger to the pulse of your potential farm along these three dimensions of farm knowledge, the more likely you will be successful in that farm.

9. **Previous Sales** – If you have sold homes in your potential farm, representing either the buyer or the seller, this is an obvious advantage. You will be able to use your proof of production in your listing presentations, your marketing materials and with potential buyers. Plus, you've proven that you can be successful in your potential farm. Nothing succeeds like success, and having already sold homes in the farm is a reliable leading indicator.

10. **Qualifying Factors** – This question is incorporated into the survey to include any qualifying factors that are not captured elsewhere in the survey that would be unique to your situation. Examples would include: Your father was the developer of the subdivision, your mother was a dominant farmer in the area, you write a real estate column in the local newspaper, you serve on the board for the PTA or some other local community organization, etc. These are just some examples of the qualifying factors that might help in your evaluation of a potential farm. The more qualifying factors you have, the more points you should allocate for this question.

Now that you have a deeper understanding of the thinking behind each of the questions, take some time to take the 10x10 Farm Evaluation Survey. And remember to be as honest as possible about each of the questions.

INTERPRETATIVE SCALE

To use the 10x10 Farm Evaluation Interpretive Scale, add up the points for the various questions in the survey and write down the total. Table 1 gives you a quick determination regarding your success potential with the farm. As with any analytical tool, you need to view the results of this survey in the broader context of your experience and unique situation. For example, if your potential farm scores low, but there is some compelling factor that overrules the result of the survey, you will have to make a more nuanced judgment regarding whether to farm the area.

Table 1: The 10x10 Farm Evaluation Survey Interpretative Scale

Total Score	Evaluation	Recommended Action
< 35	Poor Farming Potential	Consider others; only farm if a compelling factor overrules this result
36-70	Average Farming Potential	Good likelihood of success, but evaluate others for comparison; start farming if a more favorable candidate cannot be found
>70	Good Farming Potential	Outstanding opportunity, but double check answers for accuracy and bias; if legitimate, start farming immediately

Poor Farming Potential

A score below 35 points on the survey would strongly suggest that the farm is a poor candidate. While there are circumstances that would lead you to conclude that you should go ahead and farm the area, it would appear that there are few reasons to believe that it will be a productive farm for you. Keep in mind that while it may not be suited for you, it may very well be a great farm for someone else (e.g., dominant farmer, socially-connected agent, etc.).

At the very least, you should evaluate other farms for comparison purposes. You can always come back to this farm, though it will probably be unproductive in the long run.

Average Farming Potential
If your potential farm scored in the Average Farming Potential range, it indicates that this will in all likelihood be a productive farm for you. Don't be fooled by the "average" label. If you can replicate the success of an average productive farmer, you will have an outstanding real estate career. This type of score indicates that there are enough positives in this farm to justify further investigation.

Most farms that you have in mind from an intuitive perspective will fall into this range because you've already been thinking about why it would make sense on at least one dimension. While an average score indicates that this is a good farming candidate, you should still evaluate other areas to provide comparative data points. Once you're satisfied that an even better farming candidate does not exist, you should in all likelihood make the decision to start farming this area.

Good Farming Potential
If you generate a score of 70 or higher, you have truly found something special. However, I was raised to believe that if something is too good to be true, it probably isn't. I would recommend that you double-check your answers to ensure that you didn't inflate some of them because you really want to farm this area. Don't let emotionally charged motivations cloud your reasoning. In other words, if you're skewing the results

because the farm is the "prestigious" place to farm, or similar reasons, take a step back. As noted earlier, farming is expensive both from a financial and an opportunity cost perspective. Don't waste precious time and resources to satisfy your visceral motivations. On the other hand, if the score is legitimate under the cool light of reason, congratulations! You have discovered an amazingly attractive farming candidate.

Let's continue our evaluation of our hypothetical Hanover Heights farm using the 10x10 Farm Evaluation Survey.

Instructions: Circle the number that is the most appropriate answer:

1. Is there a dominant farmer and/or Is the area heavily farmed?

Heavily Farmed   Not Heavily Farmed
1   2   ③   4   5   6   7   8   9   10

2. What is the average turnover for the past three years?

As a Percentage
1   2   3   4   5   6   7   ⑧   9   10

3. Are the average prices above, below or about the same as the median for the county?

Below   About the Same   Above
1   2   3   4   5   6   ⑦   8   9   10

4. How many homes are in the farm?

100 200 300 400 500 600 700 800 900 1000+
1   2   3   ④   5   6   7   8   9   10

5. Where do you live relative to the farm?

> 5 miles   > 2.5 miles   Live in the Farm

1   2   3   4   5   6   7   8   9   ⑩

6. To what extent do you have social connections to those in the farm?

Few				Some				Numerous	
1	2	3	4	5	6	7	⑧	9	10

7. To what extent does the area have a cohesive neighborhood identity?

Little				Some				Strong	
1	2	3	4	5	6	7	⑧	9	10

8. To what extent can you identify groups of homeowners to tailor your message?

Little				Some				Strong	
1	2	3	4	5	6	7	8	⑨	10

9. How well do you know the area and how authoritatively can you discuss it?

Little Knowledge						Strong Knowledge			
1	2	3	4	5	6	⑦	8	9	10

10. How many homes have you sold in the farm already?

①	2	3	4	5	6	7	8	9	10

The total score for this farm is 65 giving it "Average Farming Potential." Looking at the various aspects of the survey, several factors stand out. One is that this agent lives in the farm. This is a very important consideration. Another is the fact that there is not an overly dominant farmer already in place.

The turnover rate is extremely high, and the pricing is also favorable. One factor that is a concern is the size of the farm.

Even if this agent is successful in her farming efforts, she will eventually reach a position of saturation.

The only way to grow the business after she has reached this position would be to grow the size of the farm. As discussed earlier, growing your farm later is not ideal because of competitive risks. However, it may be possible to farm this area and one or more adjacent areas.

Alternatively, the farmer could farm two disparate geographic farms, though this would introduce logistical and marketing message complexities. This agent should evaluate other farms for comparison, but failing a more attractive alternative, I would recommend that she start farming this area based on the 10x10 Farm Evaluation Survey.

Chapter 9 – The Farm Revenue Forecast

Once you've evaluated a potential farm using the 2x2 Farming Framework, and the 10x10 Farm Evaluation Survey, you should run the numbers in Farming Fundamental's third analytical model. The Farm Revenue Forecast will help you determine how much revenue you can expect to generate once you reach a steady state production level. Steady state means once you have ramped up your farming program and you are starting to achieve normal operating results.

This ramp up period will vary greatly by agent and by market. Some agents apply themselves more diligently and more effectively than others, and some markets are more receptive to new farmers than others. Your results will vary according to the things you can control (e.g., your effort level, your marketing program) and things you can't control (e.g., competitive response, market conditions, consumer preferences, etc.).

Here's how you run the numbers in the Farm Revenue Forecast (see Figure 4). Start with the number of homes in the farm. Multiply that by the Turnover Rate for the farm. This is the total number of homes likely to come up for sale in a given year. Multiply that value by your Target Market Share. This will give you the expected number of listings in your farm that you will list.

While you'd love to have 100% market share, it's rare for any given agent to have more than 20% market share in a farm. No matter how dominant you may become, there are an endless number of reasons why someone will pick a competitor over you. That's just life and you need to get over the fact that you won't get every listing in your farm.

Once you have calculated your expected number of listings, multiply that figure by the Average Transaction Price expected in the farm in the coming year. This will give you the gross sales for the year in the farm. Multiply that value by your Average Commission Rate to derive your expected gross commissions. Multiply your expected gross commissions by your Split to get your Net Farm Revenue.

Figure 4: Calculating Forecasted Revenue

Number of Homes in Farm
x Turnover
x Target Market Share
x Average Transaction Price
x Average Commission Rate
x Split _____
= Net Farm Revenue

Let's see how the Farm Revenue Forecast would help you determine the Net Farm Revenue for our hypothetical Hanover Heights farm. Assume your target area had the following characteristics:

Number of Homes in Farm	358
x Turnover	8.3%
x Target Market Share	15%
x Average Transaction Price	$668,000
x Average Commission Rate	3%
x Split	70%
= Net Farm Revenue	$62,524

The Farm Revenue Forecast indicates that if you achieve all of the assumptions in the model, you would expect to generate Net Farm Revenue of $62,524. Note that this number is not your take home pay. This figure does not include listing expenses (e.g., money you spend marketing the listing), and it does not include the taxes on your income. However, it does give you insight into the expected revenue in your farm.

The only way to increase your Net Farm Revenue is to change the values of the assumptions. For example, you could increase the size of the farm, or find a farm with a higher turnover rate. How to improve these points of leverage will be discussed further in Part 4 of this book.

As you think about your real estate practice, you will have several sources of business. Farming might be your primary source of business, or it may be a secondary source. Your Net Farm Revenue might be in addition to approximately $40,000 in business generated by referrals from your sphere of influence. Combined, this means that you are expecting to generate in excess of $100,000 in income.

Only you can decide if these figures are sufficient for you to make a living and to be happy in your career. The tool tells you what to expect based on assumptions. The hard work of producing the results, and whether you can live with those results, is entirely up to you.

Chapter 10 – Left-Brain Meets Right-Brain

While each of the Farm Evaluation Models are useful in isolation, reviewing all three together yields a much greater insight into the decision of whether to start farming an area. The 2x2 Farming Framework looks at what are probably the most critical factors in the attractiveness of the farm: Relative Pricing and Turnover. Also, it helps to look at the "narrative" of the farm as illustrated by the various examples given in that section.

The 10x10 Farm Evaluation Survey looks at 10 key dimensions of farming potential, and gives you a quantitative score for the farm. It is important to look beyond the raw score derived by the survey to gain insights into the various concepts behind each question. Finally, the Farm Revenue Forecast gives you the bottom line income you can expect to earn if you achieve your market share objectives in the farm.

By looking at the three models together, a clear picture regarding the viability of the farm should come into sharp focus. These analytical tools give you the quantitative view of your potential farm. You're now ready to think about the qualitative factors that might sway you one way or the other.

QUALITATIVE FACTORS

While quantitative analysis and decision-making frameworks are invaluable tools in your farm evaluation toolbox, you must also consider qualitative factors that are unique to your situation. Whereas quantitative factors have objective results (e.g., turnover rates), qualitative factors are more subjective. Each has a significant role in helping your decide where to farm. You might also think of it as your left-brain working with your right brain to come up with a best-of-both-worlds decision.

The left, or logical portion, of your brain, helps you analyze the objective measures that you can compute. The right brain is the more creative and intuitive side of your brain. Qualitative factors that can help you evaluate a farm include:

- How you feel about the architecture in the farm
- How you feel about the sub-neighborhoods in the farm
- Your opinion of the people in the farm
- How well you know the area and amenities in and around the farm
- How confident you feel about your ability to sell homes in the farm
- How knowledgeable you feel about the farm
- To what extent you feel the farm is a desirable place to live
- How you feel about the relative strengths of other agents who sell homes in the farm
- Your gut feelings about committing yourself to your farm for the next 10 years

The point of including these qualitative factors is to give yourself the opportunity to "overrule" logical and quantitative factors that may lead you to the conclusion to farm an area. In other words, if you have underlying reservations about committing to the farm that cannot be quantified, you will probably be unsuccessful. This can be as simple as your feeling that the people in the farm are unfriendly and you don't want to deal with them.

Alternatively, if the quantitative factors lead you to believe that the farm is not a viable choice, but qualifying factors argue for it, you should take those qualifying factors into consideration. Just be careful when it come to overruling quantitative factors.

You don't want to allow wishful thinking to cause you to farm an area that is a bad fit for you. If the turnover has been 2% in the farm for the past ten years, no amount of intuition is going to change the fact that very few homes will come up for sale.

As you are going to make a long-term commitment to the farm, be sure that you listen to your intuition and your true feelings and act accordingly. Just be sure that the qualitative factors you are considering are rational and legitimate. By synthesizing the logic that comes from the left side of your brain with the intuition provided by the right side of your brain, you are able to develop a balanced approach to evaluating your potential farm.

COMMITTING TO YOUR FARM
When it comes to selecting a farm, don't rush into a decision, but at the same time, don't become a victim of "paralysis by analysis." Once you've performed the exercises in the three quantitative models, and you have taken any qualitative factors into consideration, you should have a fairly clear idea regarding whether the farm will be a good candidate for you.

If, at this point, you still cannot commit to the farm, it's probably not a good candidate for you. On the other hand, there is no such thing as the perfect farm. At some point, if you are going to incorporate farming into your real estate practice, you'll have to be satisfied with finding the best choice, not the perfect choice.

Once you have made the decision to farm, you have to be mentally prepared to commit to your farm. This is not some casual commitment. This is like a marriage. If you decide to farm, you should plan on farming that farm until you retire. If you go into it half-heartedly, or you take a wait-and-see approach, you will not be successful, and you will waste precious time and financial resources.

You need to be able to withstand the lack of production you will inevitably experience when you are starting up in the farm. You need to allocate the necessary time and financial resources required to farm effectively. It won't be easy, it won't be cheap and it might not work out.

So, if you've been trolling around looking for the latest silver bullet, or you need a quick fix for your business before you go back to looking for a "real job," farming is not the answer. This is for real estate professionals who understand the sacrifice and dedication that is required to be great, and who are willing to commit to a program until it works.

If you have the passion and stick-to-itiveness needed to be a successful farmer, and you have identified your farm, proceed to Part 3 to start the next phase of your real estate career.

Part 3 – How to Farm

"Being busy does not always mean real work. The object of all work is production or accomplishment and to either of these ends there must be forethought, system, planning, intelligence, and honest purpose, as well as perspiration. Seeming to do is not doing."

—— Thomas Edison

This section is a nuts and bolts description of the activities you will need to perform to be successful in your farm. As you read this section, remember that though you will perform these activities in your own way, you must remain true to these farming activities to be successful. If you decide not to perform all of these activities, or if you deviate significantly from them, your farming effectiveness will suffer. Farming is a way of life, and it will take time for these activities to become second nature. The activities described in this section will put you on the path to becoming a successful farmer.

Chapter 11 – Do These Three Things

There are three activities that are far and away the most important to your success as a farmer and a real estate agent: Prospecting, accumulating product knowledge and gathering market knowledge. Everything else on your to do list should take a back seat to these critical areas.

PROSPECTING
Prospecting is all about creating a consistent source of business. You know that if you wait for your pipeline to dry up before your start prospecting, you will have a dangerous gap in business that could be fatal to your real estate practice. That is why consistent prospecting is by far the most important use of your time.

The rule of thumb that most sales professionals use is to devote two solid hours to prospecting per working day. This may not sound like a lot of time, but if you work six days a week, that is 12 hours of prospecting each week. That amount of prospecting will lead to transactions, and transactions lead to additional business from neighbors and referrals.

However, if you slack off, your pipeline will never achieve productive status. This rule of thumb also makes it more likely that you will actually prospect every day. If you are not able to make this minimal commitment, you are unlikely to succeed in real estate sales.

Keep in mind that prospecting is not about activities like returning calls to existing clients or other real estate professionals. It refers to all the prospecting activities that actually lead to new business. This can be any number of lead generation activities. The key from a Time Management standpoint is to carve out time on your calendar to actually perform the activity. Whether you use the time to door knock, write personal notes to past clients or make follow up calls to buyer leads from your open house, only use the time to prospect. If you need to, put a sign on your desk or office that reads, "Do Not Disturb – I am Prospecting" so other agents know to leave you alone.

Most agents carve out time for prospecting in the mid morning hours when they and their prospects are fresh. I personally recommend 9:30 am to 11:30am for prospecting, even for door knocking (studies have shown that one third of homeowners are home during the day). This allows you time in the morning to take care of necessary evils like checking email and voicemail, and it gives your prospects time to recover from the morning rush.

When you're done, you can break for lunch and then you have the remainder of the day to do things like touring properties, calling existing clients, showing property, completing paperwork, creating property flyers, etc.

PRODUCT KNOWLEDGE
Product Knowledge is how well you know the location, condition, features and relative value of properties in your coverage area. If you showed up at a Ford dealer and the sales person couldn't tell you how the Taurus compared to the Camry, you'd probably find another dealer.

Consumers are fickle, and they also have seemingly unlimited information at their fingertips. If you are not intimately familiar with the properties they may be considering, they'll probably find someone else to represent them (buyer or seller).

You build product knowledge by personally previewing the homes in your coverage area. Looking at the photos online is not a substitute. For one thing, real estate photographs tend not to include any negative features that may existing in or around the home.

Seeing the house in person also gives you so much more sensory information. You'll get information on the odors that may exist in the house. You'll see whether there are any sources of noise that may influence buyers. You'll see the condition of homes (and landscaping) near the house you are previewing. You might see and even chat with the neighbors who will give you insight. You'll get an idea regarding how traffic affects access to and from the home.

I suggest taking notes about the properties you preview so you can share your thoughts with potential buyers and sellers. One way to do this is to print out the data sheet from the MLS of all the homes you're going to preview. You can write notes on the back of the data sheets.

When a property is sold, you can archive it for future reference or recycle the data sheet. Writing notes will also help you remember details more readily. If you do this (and tour properties regularly), I promise you that you will have better product knowledge than 80% of your competitors.

Today, you can also take pictures, video and notes (either written or recorded audio) of previewed homes on your smart phone or tablet that you can use for your knowledge or to share with clients.

Regardless of your methodology, remember that consumers are looking for you to be the expert regarding the inventory on the market. Previewing homes is not something you do when you have time. You need to carve out time for it each week to stay current with the products you could be selling.

MARKET KNOWLEDGE

Just as you need to have in-depth product knowledge, you also must have timely market knowledge. You need to be able to pass the cocktail party test. Imagine you're at a cocktail party and you are introduced to someone you've never met. During the course of some small talk, the person asks you what you do. You tell them you sell real estate. After a brief pause the inevitable happens and he asks, "So, how's the market?" If you don't have a ready answer for this at all times, you may as well tell them that you're thinking about getting into real estate.

Passing the cocktail party test means being able to convey market statistics, news events and market trends in a way that is accessible yet authoritative. In order to do this, you need to spend the time to gather knowledge about what's going on in the market on a variety of dimensions (in decreasing order of importance):

- Market statistics
- Market trends
- Interest rates and lending practices
- Real estate news
- Economic news

Market Statistics

The most important information you must possess has to do with market statistics for your coverage area. At a minimum, this includes your farm, but it also pertains to the broader coverage area in which you do business.

You should be able to quote (from memory) the level of inventory, whether the inventory level is increasing or decreasing, the number of sales in the past week, the number of sales in the past month, whether sales are increasing, steady or decreasing, the average days on market, how many homes have had price reductions, the number of homes that have received multiple offers, open house activity, etc.

Market Trends

The next area has to do with the macro trends that are affecting the local market. These include whether employers are hiring or laying off workers, the level of new home construction in your area, the improving quality of schools in your area, whether the population is increasing or decreasing in your area, etc.

Trends like these are unique to your area, and they have a direct effect on the housing market. As such, you should have a working understanding of these trends.

Interest Rates and Lending Practices

As interest rates are so intimately tied to the housing market, you need to be able to quote current interest rates associated with various lending products. You also need to have a working knowledge of lending practices that can affect your transactions. Avoid overkill on these topics and refer your clients to a specialist when the conversation starts to go deep.

Real Estate and Economic News

Don't become a news junky just in case someone asks you about Assembly Bill 385 that is currently working its way through the state legislature (unless it is something material like limiting the mortgage interest deduction). However, if there are big news stories going on in real estate or in the general economy that affect real estate, you should be conversant in those stories.

How do you gather all of this information? There are numerous sources for gathering this information. Market statistics should be readily available from your board, association or brokerage firm. There are also numerous sources of market statistics available online. You also need to talk with other agents to gather information about the market. Be ready and willing to share the information you have. The collective sharing of information within the local real estate community is one of the best things real estate professionals can do for one another.

You should also attend your office meeting to hear anecdotes and to gather market information. Read and watch the news from a variety of news source, whether online, on TV or in print.

Your job is to take all this information in, synthesize it in your mind so that you understand it, and then practice discussing it with other people in a conversational and advisory manner. This is something you can role-play with other agents, your spouse, your friends, etc.

You won't be authoritative from day one, but remember that the people you are talking to are not as knowledgeable about the market as you are. Confidence is as important as the actual information, but confidence is gained from taking the time to absorb and synthesize the information.

Chapter 12 – Your Business Plan

Every business has a plan. Some businesses have poorly-conceived plans, and others have innovative and highly successful plans. Some business plans are written, but most are not. Most business owners don't take the time to think their business plan through very thoroughly, let alone put it in writing. As a result, many businesses survive, but underperform, and it explains why more than half of small businesses fail in the first four years of existence.

Whether you're an independent contractor working for a national brokerage or an independent broker working under your own license, you're running your own business. And you're in the business of sales. You need a business plan that will help you achieve your sales goals.

Many agents don't create a business plan because they find false comfort in telling themselves that they're too busy to create a plan. I don't think I have to tell you that when you're in the real estate business, you'll always be busy! If you think you're too busy to create a business plan and you're not achieving your sales goals, you're probably spending a lot of your time on busy work.

Busy work is any activity that can be construed by an outside observer to look like work, but that doesn't actually help you meet your sales goals. Examples include tinkering with your website, spending hours working on a property flyer, researching loan programs, etc.

If you don't have a business plan, you're probably relying on intuition, or you're doing things as you've always done them, or your emulating (i.e., copying) your perception of someone else's plan. It's kind of like jumping in the car for a long road trip and neglecting to bring a map or navigation device. Playing things by ear is fine for a weekend excursion, but it's unacceptable for a business owner.

If you want your business to be successful, you need to create a plan that has the following elements:

1. Sales Goals
2. Marketing Strategy
3. Marketing Budget
4. Time Management Plan

Chapter 13 – Sales Goals

In the farm evaluation section, you saw how to calculate the forecasted revenue for your farm. Based on your desired revenue goal, you can then ascertain how many sales you need to achieve to meet that revenue goal.

Let's start with an example of a hypothetical farm. Assume your target area had the following characteristics:

Number of Homes in Farm	728
x Turnover	6%
x Target Market Share	15%
x Average Transaction Price	$548,000
x Average Commission Rate	3%
x Split	70%
= Net Farm Revenue	$75,400

Assuming turnover is relatively constant and that will you hit your target market share, you will need to generate at least seven transactions in your farm (728 x 6% = 43.68 potential transactions in your farm x 15% market share = 6.5). Note that if you need to round this up to seven to make sure you meet your revenue goal (and the fact that you can't sell part of a house!).

Note that this can also be viewed as "sides" of a transaction. For example, if you have six listings in your farm, and you double end one of them, you still generate the equivalent of seven individual transactions.

Now that you know that you need to generate at least seven transactions in your farm, you need to create a plan to achieve that goal. In order to get seven listings, you need to secure more than seven listing appointments.

The average agent wins approximately one out of three listings in competitive conditions. In other words, situations in which you're competing head to head with other agents. The good news is that sometimes they only call you and you're not competing with other agents. However, under normal circumstances, you will not close all the deals for which you interview. Luckily, you can do things to improve your win ratio like making your listing presentation more effective.

What this means is that if you're doing a decent job on your listing appointments, you'll need to go on three listing appointments to get one listing. If your goal is to land seven listings, you'll need to go on at least 21 listing appointments during the year.

To meet your sales goals, you need to figure out how to get those listing appointments. You'll need to hustle to get those appointments. As your experience grows and your brand recognition builds, and you start to generate more proof of production, you'll find it easier to get listing appointments.

As a farmer, your number one job is to maximize the number of listing appointments you put on your calendar. To a certain extent, everything else is busy work. To get 21 listing appointments in a year, you'll need to average approximately two appointments per month. In summary, your sales goals can be describe as follows:

- Total number of projected sales in farm = 7
- Average win ratio on listings appointments 1/3
- Total listing appointments needed = 21
- Average transaction price in my farm to remain steady at $548,000
- Forecasted revenue from farm = $75,400

Once you establish your sales goals, you can move on to your marketing strategy.

Chapter 14 – Marketing Strategy

Your marketing strategy is your plan for penetrating your target market. The plan is composed of the following elements:

Step 1: Market Analysis
Step 2: Segmentation
Step 3: Positioning
Step 4: Marketing Communications Plan

STEP 1: MARKET ANALYSIS
The first step is to perform an analysis of your market. This will come partly from the work you performed when you were evaluating potential farms. The difference here is to ascertain the motivating factors that homeowners in your farm exhibit that will enable you to position yourself and to create marketing messages that resonate with them. In other words, what do they care about, and how can you satisfy those concerns?

For example, if you dig deeper into your farm and you discover that most of the owners in the area are seniors living in empty nest circumstances, your marketing messages will be very different than for young, single professionals.

In addition to your own primary market research based on your direct interaction with the people in the farm, you should perform secondary research on your farm and really understand the demographic composition of the farm. There are many sources of demographic information available online that you can find by searching on the term "demographic." Some of the best information can be found using basic census information available for free from the government (See: census.gov).

You will find this information to be both fascinating and informative. Don't attempt to create a demographic profile for every homeowner in your farm. Just use the information to create broad profiles that will help you segment your market. A sample market analysis might look something like the following:

Sample Market Analysis: *"Sunset Oaks is a master planned community built in the 1970's situated around a large park filled with heritage oak trees and a small lake. The park is a major recreational draw for area residents. The homes in the area are considered to be larger than average, and many young families have moved into the neighborhood to take advantage of the bigger homes and good schools.*

Many of the original and long-time owners are now empty nesters, and many of them are retiring to another master planned community nearby that caters to seniors with both on-site health care and recreational activities.

Approximately 60% of Sunset Oaks residents are original or long-time owners with 40% being young families. Long-time residents have income levels below the median for the region, though they also have the most equity in their homes.

They are also most likely to identify themselves as being affiliated with an organized religion and they are most likely to vote. Young families moving into Sunset Oaks have incomes above the median for the region.

As newer homeowners, they are less likely to have significant equity in their homes. They tend not to identify themselves as being affiliated with an organized religion, are less likely to vote and are more likely to take vacations out of state."

It may seem like a waste of time to delve this deeply into the makeup of your farm, but performing this simple exercise will make you more of an authority on the area and, more importantly, it will inform how to segment your market.

STEP 2: SEGMENTATION
Once you've identified the type of farm that you think makes the most sense for you, you might consider one last refinement to your farming approach. A farm consists of unique people and families, each with a unique background and set of circumstances that led them to live in your potential farm.

While it is possible to find a farm that is almost completely homogenous, most neighborhoods are comprised of a mixture of different types of people. A homogenous farm might be an area of a city that has a lot of older warehouses converted to live-work loft spaces. These homes would likely attract homeowners who are very similar in their demographic and psychographic profiles. Condominium projects would also tend to have homeowners who are similar to one another.

More commonly, you will find neighborhoods that are more heterogeneous in composition. For example, you may have older couples with grown children who might be classified as Empty Nesters. If the neighborhood attracted people 25 years ago as a good place to raise children, chances are that there might be a sizable number of young families who have moved into the area.

The motivations of these two groups of homeowners will in all probability be very different from one another. Empty nesters who are retired with grown children in another part of the country will often be motivated to move because they want a smaller home with less maintenance. Perhaps they love their home, but they just want to be near their children and grandchildren. A young family might love their home, but they need to move because of a job transfer.

Alternately, the young families who are most likely to move due to a job change might be most interested in learning about the relocation services you or your company offers, or about your referral network of agents in other parts of the country.

When you identify the unique needs of potential prospects, your marketing should speak specifically to the motivations of your targeted homeowners. The process of separating groups of homeowners into categories with shared traits is called Segmentation.

The practice of communicating a specific message to a group of prospects with similar characteristics is called Target Marketing. You might decide that your marketing budget would best be spent only targeting empty nesters because they have an elevated probability of selling. In addition, you might be SRES® accredited meaning that you specialize in issues specific to seniors.

You will be able to stretch your marketing dollar further if you are able to identify specific traits in your potential farm, segment your prospects based on shared traits, and then target your marketing with specific messaging that resonates with that group.

In most cases, your market will be composed of a variety of different types of groups. Segmentation is simply the process of separating people into groups with shared characteristics. By doing so, a marketer is better able to craft a message that will be meaningful to a given group. In the Sunset Oaks example, segmenting the market will be very straightforward. In that farm, you have empty nesters and young families.

As a farmer, you are faced with the decision of whether to market to both groups, or just one of the two. However, by understanding the differences between the two groups, you can determine whether and when to communicate different messages. In some cases, the message may be the same. For example, sending a "Season's Greetings" postcard would be appropriate for both groups.

How you segment your market is limited only by your imagination. How granular you go depends on the information you have available, your interest level and how important it is to your sales goals. Demographic information is widely available. Psychographic information is harder to access, but can provide great insights.

Once you have a clear understanding of the market segments you want to market to, you'll need a prospecting list. There are numerous sources for obtaining lists of prospects, and they often provide many filters to help you drill down to just the prospects you want. For example, you may apply the following filters to generate your prospect list:

Homeowners...
who live in the Sunset Oaks sub-division
who are at least 60 years old
who have lived in their home for more than 10 years
who have household income of at least $35,000

This is a highly targeted type of list, and you may not find it necessary to drill down this deeply. Perhaps you just need to use the last sale date of the property to help you segment long time owners from more recent arrivals. Many companies offer comprehensive databases of homeowners and can provide some level of filtering to help you create a targeted prospecting list.

STEP 3: POSITIONING
You will create a marketing plan to communicate your value proposition to your target market. In this case, the product you are marketing is you and the services you provide. You should

start by thinking about how you'll be positioning yourself and your services. You should then write out your positioning statement so that you stay on track with your marketing communications. A positioning statement regarding you would be something like the following:

Sample Positioning Statement: *"To achieve my sales goals, I will position myself as a local expert who has deep local knowledge that comes from living in the area for the last 5 years and being involved in the community. I will further position myself as a consummate professional in whom you would place a high-degree of trust similar to that of an attorney helping you with your estate planning.*

My marketing objective is that if you're a homeowner in my farm and you're thinking about selling, you think of me and invite me to interview for the job because of your perception of my local knowledge and professionalism."

There are many other possibilities when it comes to how you may position yourself. This will evolve into your brand over time. Your brand should be an accurate reflection of your true persona and the type of service you deliver.

In other words, if you position yourself as the tech savvy agent, and you show up to a listing appointment with a printed listing presentation and not a laptop or tablet, your positioning doesn't match your reality. This will create a disconnect in the minds of your potential clients and will lead them to eliminate you more easily.

Think about the type of agent you are (and aspire to be) and then create a positioning statement that reflects your emerging brand. Additional examples include positioning yourself as:

- The marketing guru that will market your client's home most effectively
- The tech savvy agent who knows how to use all the latest technology tools and services
- The experienced negotiator who will get the best deal for you
- The "folksy" agent who you'll love to work with (think of agents who have their dog with them in their portrait photo)
- The agent with the sense of humor (think of the agent who puts the "Honey, Stop the Car!" rider on their listing
- The agent who has sold the most homes in the area (although you probably wouldn't be reading this book if that was the case, but keep this one in mind for later!)

STEP 4: MARKETING COMMUNICATIONS PLAN

Once you have decided how you will position your personal brand, you will create a messaging statement that will resonate with your target audience(s).

Sample Messaging Statement: *"Sunset Oaks is composed of empty nesters and young families. For empty nesters, I will provide information regarding issues that matter to seniors including retirement community options, property tax issues, etc. For young families, I will provide information that they would find beneficial including information on local schools, recreation programs, relocation services, etc. Marketing messages that would be meaningful for both groups include information about market conditions, current events in the area, etc. In all cases, my messaging will position myself as the consummate real estate professional."*

In order to communicate your message to your target audience(s), you will need to create a comprehensive marketing communications plan. There are many vehicles that can facilitate your communications, but you will have to prioritize them based on several criteria:

1. **Effectiveness** – You must ensure that any communications vehicle you employ can be demonstrated to be effective. In other words, is there a positive Return on Investment (ROI) on your marketing expenditure? Placing a print ad in the local newspaper may make you feel like a legitimate real estate professional, but you have to ascertain whether it actually helps you achieve your marketing strategy. Also, if that same ad makes sense as part of a larger marketing program, it may be perfectly justifiable.

2. **Appropriateness** – If you are positioning yourself as the real estate professional serving Gen Y loft owners in an urban setting, you probably want to make sure that social media is an important component of your marketing communication plan. However, if your target market is senior homeowners in a mature suburban neighborhood, you probably don't want to try to reach your audience this way. A toll-free number to receive a local market report by mail might be more appropriate for this audience. Make sure that your communications channel meets your target audience where they are, and how they like to communicate.

3. **Budget Considerations** – In addition to effectiveness and appropriateness, you need to make sure that you take the required budget into consideration. If you decide that taking out bus stop ads is the best way to reach your target audience, you need to research the cost of those ads and allocate the associated budget to that marketing channel.

Keep in mind that budget can refer to hard dollar cash cost, but it can also refer to the time you spend on creating and maintaining your marketing channel. For example, if you decide that using Twitter®, Facebook® and YouTube® is how you're going to address your target audience, you have to budget the significant time that it will take to maintain those channels.

When blogging first became available, many real estate practitioners wrote a few blog entries and then stopped because they got busy, didn't know what to write about or didn't see immediate results.

Many of these so-called "free" marketing channels require significant investments of time. If you choose one or more of these channels, budget your time in terms of dollars to measure your ROI.

You can do this by taking your expected farm revenue and dividing by 2080 hours. This is the number of standard working hours in a year, and it's a good reminder that you should stay focused on the 20% of activities that deliver 80% of the results. In our example, this would translate into $36.25 per hour ($75,400 divided by 2080). If you spend 3 hours per day maintaining your social media channels, your daily cost is $108.75 (3 hours x $36.25).

MARKETING COMMUNICATIONS CHANNELS

There are many marketing communications ("marcomm") channels available to a marketer. This section describes some of the marcomm channels and how they might fit into your specific marketing program. Keep in mind that combining multiple communications channels increases awareness by reinforcing messages from other channels. This increased awareness is the first step in generating leads from your farm.

Direct Mail – Direct mail remains an effective marcomm channel for farmers. This holds true despite the rise of social media and the plethora of online communications channels available. In fact, it probably is more effective now precisely because so many consumers are experiencing burnout from overexposure to online communications channels on their computers, tablets and smart phones.

Direct mail is effective because it is tangible and it must be physically handled. This means that it has a greater likelihood of remaining in the possession of your prospect. Moreover, direct mail in your prospects' hands is better able to break through the marketing noise in their life.

Direct mail is also effective for farming precisely because it is not opt-in. In other words, unless you have asked not to receive direct mail, I can target you and get my message delivered to you.

In my research, I have found that the best practice in direct mail for farming is to use a call-to-action that provides the consumer with the information they want, in a way that puts the consumer in control of the situation. They can then engage you when they are ready, and on their own terms. I recommend using direct mail to draw people to your website where you can fulfill a call-to-action that has relevance and meaning for your target audience.

The most important aspect of your farming program is to be consistent. You will want to mail to your farm at least once a month. Twice a month is better if you can afford it and you want to see results sooner. Your mail program should look something like:

- January – Farming Postcard
- February – Farming Postcard
- March – Quarterly Newsletter
- April – Farming Postcard
- May – Farming Postcard
- June – Quarterly Newsletter
- July – Farming Postcard
- August – Farming Postcard
- September – Quarterly Newsletter
- October – Farming Postcard
- November – Farming Postcard
- December – Quarterly Newsletter or Annual Report

The farming postcards can be tailored to fit the time of year either from a real estate perspective (e.g., Spring Selling Season), or from a seasonal standpoint (e.g., Season's Greetings).

You can also substitute proof of production content, as there is no better way to get additional listings than to be perceived as a success in the local market.

The newsletters should provide relevant information about the local real estate market. Don't make it too complex, and don't make it too corny. Remember that most homeowners simply care about what homes are selling around them, what they're going for and who's selling them. As you're sending the information, many will assume that you're the one selling them.

Local Phone Number Magnet – Send a magnet to your farm that includes useful phone numbers for your local area. This can be for the local pharmacy, the most popular restaurant, the attendance number for the local school, etc.

For whatever reason, people find it very hard to throw away magnets. They almost always end up on the refrigerator. Once on the fridge, you'll probably be there for years – your smiling face beaming night and day in their kitchen. The local numbers probably won't get used much, but people will think they're useful, and it also positions you as a local expert.

Calendars – Like magnets, calendars are something that consumers just can't seem to bring themselves to throw away. Send these out or distribute them by door knocking in December for the upcoming year. The timing is perfect, because the spring selling season is just around the corner.

If you send a calendar with attractive imagery (in addition to your portrait, of course), your chances of ending up on the wall somewhere in the house are good. This marketing piece will promote you for the next 12 months for a good proportion of your farm.

Once you have your base farming program organized, you can determine whether and how to use additional marketing communications channels. Each of the following provides unique benefits and limitations, but the more ways you promote yourself, the faster you'll build your brand and your production level.

Print Ads
While many pundits have written off print ads entirely, the smart marketer evaluates his or her situation independently and lets the facts direct the decision. While print ads are often

expensive and hard to track from a Return on Investment standpoint, it can be a cost-effective marketing communications channel under the right circumstances.

In the town where I practice real estate, it seems like virtually everyone in town reads the local newspaper. Note that this is not the major regional newspaper. The smaller, highly localized papers can be a good forum to build your brand.

On the other hand, placing an ad in the open house section of the paper is rapidly becoming obsolete as this information is becoming ubiquitous online. However, try explaining why your client's home is not included in the open house guide! Ads in property magazines likewise serve no practical sales purpose as listing info is universally available online and on smart phones. Even though these types of ads don't really sell homes, they do promote your proof of production and your commitment to marketing properties in a variety of media outlets.

Signage
Signage is by far the best bang for the marketing buck. Yard signs, open house directional signs and riders all have long useful lives, are relatively inexpensive and provide you with low-cost advertising when you display them in your farm area (they only cost you your time to put them out). I would recommend getting as many open house directional signs as you can afford. When you have an open house, blanket the area so neighbors and farm residents remember your name from all the repetition. They'll also think you're selling a lot of properties in the area.

In addition, you should consider creating riders for your yard signs that advertise you as a local expert for that specific neighborhood. You might also create riders that advertise a specific listing with a Property URL (PURL), provided you have a single property website, virtual tour or other online destination page. An example would be a sign with "Virtual Tour: www.2063Mayfield.com" printed on it.

Finally, a rider with a smart phone tag that would direct consumers to this type of destination website would also be a good way to drive potential buyers to you. This is especially useful in cases when you have a flyer box and you run out of property flyers.

Open House
When you consider the three key constituencies that come to an open house, you quickly realize how important an open house can be to your real estate practice. The three groups are neighbors, potential buyers and other agents. An open house is both an opportunity to sell your listing and to leverage that listing to generate additional business.

Even when a neighbor comes to your open house and proclaims that they are just a "nosy neighbor," you should be grateful for their presence. Neighbors are simply sellers in waiting. By coming to your open house, you have the opportunity to establish rapport, and to probe for possible motivations to sell.

They may tell you that they are getting ready to sell now, or they may tell you that "they'll have to carry me out of my house in a pine box," or they may tell you something in between. Neighbors also may be able to provide you with buyer referrals from their sphere of influence. No matter their situation, meeting neighbors is your best way to build your contact base in your farm.

When you conduct an open house, your job is, of course, to sell the home you are holding open. This is true whether or not you are the listing agent. If you are the listing agent, and you find a buyer for the home, you'll double end the deal and make twice the commission. Obviously, you have a high degree of motivation to find a buyer under those circumstances. For all agents, open house is the perfect way to establish relationships with buyers to represent them in the sale of other homes, hopefully in your farm.

Finally, meeting other agents at your open houses will enable you to build relationships in your local agent community, engage in information-sharing about the local market and persuade agents to bring their clients to your listing. While you are in competition with other agents, you will need to work well with the agents in your area to be successful.

Door Knocking
Many agents have mixed feelings about door knocking. While most agents would recognize the importance of door knocking, it is something that most agents find distasteful. Performing a general door knock in your farm is time-consuming and likely to increase your dislike for this activity.

Many agents who muster the courage to door knock try to do a huge amount of homes, they burn out and then quickly abandon the tactic. Therefore, if you can segment your door knocking so that your it will be more effective and rewarding, you'll be more likely to stick with it in the long run.

One of the best ways to practice door knocking is to invite neighbors to an open house. This is a non-threatening way to introduce yourself and to invite neighbors to something of potential interest to them. Remember that it's always a good idea to bring something of value when you door knock. This can be a marketing giveaway like a notepad, or it can be something of informational value like a local market activity report.

Blogging
Blogging can be a very effective way to reach your target audience. There are many ways to get involved with blogging,

from writing long, thoughtful articles, to recording videos about the local market, to micro-blogging using tools like Twitter. When you consider blogging, keep in mind that anything you publish online could be available forever. So don't publish anything that you may possibly regret in the future.

Your best bet is to stick to professional content about market activity, statistics, articles about owning and maintaining a home, and useful information for buyers and sellers. The other thing to keep in mind is that this will only be an effective communication channel if you publish consistently.

Social Media
One of the best ways to stay connected to your sphere of influence is to be active with a variety of social media tools. Suffice it to say that social media will only grow as an important component of the marketing communications mix.

Craigslist and Listing Syndication
When you want to promote a listing, you can utilize listing syndication platforms that disseminate your listing information to a variety of property search sites. Listing syndication sites will distribute your listings to sites like Trulia®. They'll also give you the ability to post formatted ads on Craigslist. These free sites are a great way to promote your listings online and to reach additional buyer leads.

Pay Per Click Ads
Search Engine Marketing (SEM) gives you the ability to advertise to a targeted group of buyers and sellers in your geographic area. Pay per click ads are what made Google a multi-billion dollar company. Your ad appears when someone searches for key words that you've sponsored.

You pay the search engine company (Yahoo and Microsoft have similar programs) when someone clicks on your ad (hence, pay per click). When the click the ad, they are taken to the website embedded in the ad and this is known as a click through.

You don't pay anything when your ad is displayed in a search result and the user does not click through. These are known as impressions, and they act like little banner ads for your business. When you sponsor pay per click ads, you can set a not-to-exceed budget (e.g., $10 per day).

When you're getting started, be sure to manage your budget carefully so your costs don't spiral out of control. If you're farming a location, you might try placing an ad for terms that would be used by buyers, sellers or both. For example, if you were farming the Monta Vista area of Cupertino, you could sponsor terms like, "Cupertino real estate," "Monta Vista real estate," "Monta Vista realtor," etc.

Your Website
Creating and maintaining a professional website for your real estate practice is essential for success. A website is essentially an online resume that your prospects will research when they're deciding whether to work with you. If your website positions you as an expert serving your local farm area, potential sellers will be comforted by your focus on their neighborhood. You might also have a separate website with your name as the URL to target your sphere of influence.

In addition to your online resume, your website should fulfill your direct marketing calls to action, either from your direct mail programs, your online promotions or your email marketing programs. Converting prospects into leads is the main purpose of your website, and your website should make it easy to fulfill a call to action or to get in contact with you.

In addition, your website should do a credible job of demonstrating your proof of production. Featured listings and buyer-represented sales should be promoted heavily on your website. You should also consider producing a market activity blog or video blog that will improve your search engine rankings and provide value-added information for your farm prospects.

This can be as simple as providing a weekly update on how many new listings came to the market, how many went pending and some recent sales data. You can supplement this with anecdotal information like how busy open houses were the previous weekend. If you can do this on a consistent basis, it will both bear fruit for you and force you to stay on top of market conditions in your farm area.

Events
Promoting events in your market area will help build your brand and put you in touch with homeowners who live in your farm. Ideas for local events include sponsoring existing events like walk-a-thons at your local elementary school, to creating your own events like a summer ice cream social at the local park. Philanthropic events are another great way to give back to society while building relationships in your community. If there is no other motive than to create or participate in a fun atmosphere, it will give you invaluable time to build rapport with your farming prospects.

Giveaways
Whether you send them by mail, door knock with them or give them to individuals as you meet them, giveaways are a proven method of building awareness in your farm. Be strategic in your marketing giveaway spending as you can easily burn a big hole in your marketing budget on trinkets and trash. Items of value that people will actually keep will help build your brand, especially if you are known for something.

Chapter 15 – Marketing Budget

While there are prospecting methods that enable you to exchange your time instead of spending money on marketing, farming requires that you spend money to be effective. The big question is how much you'll need to spend to achieve your sales goals.

The general rule of thumb in marketing is that you need to spend approximately 10% of your projected gross sales on marketing. Therefore, if your sales goal is $250,000 in gross commission income, you'll need to spend approximately $25,000 on marketing.

If that sounds like a lot of money, it is. Moreover, spending the money doesn't necessarily mean that you'll be successful. That's called risk and there is no way to manage risk down to zero (unless, of course, you get out of the business). If you look at the number and it gives you an anxiety attack, you're probably not cut out for farming. Just remember that if you achieve that type of sales goal, you'll be a top producer, and it's not easy, or cheap, to be a top producer.

The good news is that you won't have to pay all that money up front. You'll be able to spread out your marketing expenditures over time, presumably as you're closing deals along the way to help fund your marketing program.

Let's take a look at how you would construct your marketing budget. Let's continue the example from the Sales Goals section in which you have a farm size of 728 and you expect to get seven listings on a steady state basis. Assuming you use the direct marketing approach described earlier, you can expect to spend the following for your annual marketing expense (adjust the cost of the mailings as postage rates increase):

FARMING MARKETING EXPENSE

Farm Size	728
Price per Mailing	$0.59
Cost Per Mailing	$430
Number of Mailings	12
Direct Mail Expense	$5,154

You'll also need to spend money to promote your listings. The good news is that this proof of production activity will help you generate additional listings. Additional listings will also help you prospect for buyer clients. For seven listings, you might expect to spend the following to promote the listing and leverage it to gain additional clients (figures for illustration purposes only):

LISTING MARKETING EXPENSE

Signage ($25 for riders)	$175
Flyers ($49 per listing)	$343
Virtual Tours ($79 per listing)	$553
Proof of Production Mailers ($430 per mailing)	$3,007
Total Listing Expense	$4,078

Adding your two marketing expenses brings you to a total of $9,232 for the year. This represents 12.2% of your projected farm revenue of $75,400. Let's look at how this breaks down per listing:

Net revenue per listing	$10,771
Farming Expense per listing	$736
Listing Expense per listing	$583
Total Marketing Expense per listing	$1,319
Profit per Listing	$9,453
Return on Investment	717%

These numbers are incredible! How many businesses or investments do you know of that generate 717% return on investment? Compare this to a retail establishment that requires investment in inventory, an expensive retail lease, employee wages and employment taxes, inventory shrinkage from shoplifting and employee theft, liability insurance, overhead, etc. This says nothing of the intense competition you would face.

Even most service business models can't touch the returns associated with farming. If you were billing your services out at $50 an hour, you would have to work for 216 hours to generate $10,771 in billings. That's the equivalent of 27 eight-hour workdays. If you worked five days a week, eight hours a day, it would take you 5½ weeks of solid work to generate those billings.

As you contemplate these numbers, keep in mind that this is based on your net revenue after your split (30% to the broker in this example). Also, you will be generating additional transactions from buyer clients that you cultivate by promoting these listings. In addition, your market share will grow over time if you are successful, so this marketing budget will decline as a percentage of gross revenue.

How do you start farming if you don't have any money? If you're convinced that farming is for you, but you don't have the money, you can employ other prospecting methods that allow you to exchange your time instead of spending money on marketing. Once you close a couple of transactions, set funds aside to start your farming program. This is known as the bootstrapping method of farming and it's how most farmers get started.

Chapter 16 – Time Management Plan

Even the best marketing plan will fail in the absence of a successful Time Management Plan. Never forget that time is a valuable commodity. Your time is more precious than even your money. Why? A dollar is worth a dollar and it will still be worth a dollar tomorrow (ignoring inflation). On the other hand, time has several interesting properties that make it more complex than money.

The first has to do with the perishability of time. Much like an airline can't have a clearance sale on empty seats on past flights, you can't recover hours wasted on busy work and other unproductive tasks.

Another important property of time is that it is finite in nature. As a normal, mortal human being, you are granted a fixed number of hours in which to live. Assuming that you live to be 75, you have exactly 657,000 hours on this planet. Unfortunately, you can't go to the store and buy more time.

Compare that to money. There is no limit to how much money you can possess, and it is unrelated to age. A 24-year-old technologist can be a billionaire, and an 80-year-old plumber who has worked hard all his life can be penniless. While money can create great disparities, time is the great equalizer in life.

Finally, there is the opportunity cost of time. Think of opportunity cost in the following way. When you get a traditional wage-earning job, you are trading your time in exchange for your wages. When a company is paying you, you forego other opportunities and perform the tasks they ask of you during work hours.

Setting aside for a moment the pervasive myth of multi-tasking, you can't do more than one thing with your time at once. You can either complain to your broker about the transaction that fell through, or you can spend that time prospecting, but you can't do both at the same time. Whenever you engage in an activity, you are making a judgment that you are foregoing an opportunity to do something else. That is why it is so critical to ensure that your time is spent productively.

Let's consider an example regarding the choices we make about how we spend our time. Let's say that you were given the choice of going to the weekly broker's meeting to hear a speaker talk about the new laws related to the title industry. You'll also hear about new listings on the market that will help build your product knowledge.

Your second choice is to attend a referral group meeting facilitated by the local chamber of commerce. If you described either of these to a friend outside the industry, they would both seem like valid work-related activities. So, which choice would you make?

This is known as a leading question. Of course, you say you'll attend the referral group. Well, now let's introduce a new wrinkle. In the referral group, you're expected to provide at least one solid referral to a member of your group each week. You don't have a referral for any of them for the third consecutive week and it will be a slightly uncomfortable meeting for that reason.

Now which meeting are you likely to attend? This twist points to the fact that the degree to which the activities take us out of our comfort zone often dictates how we make decisions about our time.

For all these reasons, I believe that time is more valuable than money. So how should you make decisions about the use of your time? I have found that the easiest way to make this judgment is to ask yourself the following question: "If I had to pay someone to perform this activity, would it be worth the expense?" If you ask yourself this question consistently, you will start to eliminate busy work and idle time and you will be on your way to a more productive career.

TIME MANAGEMENT TRAPS

Most agents know what they should be doing, but it's obviously easier said than done. However, the longer you put off doing the right things, the longer it's going to take to reach your goals. If you don't create a comprehensive Time Management plan, you may fall into a variety of Time Management Traps:

Spending time on busy work – As noted earlier, busy work is composed of activities that look like work, but don't produce results (i.e., the 80% of activities that produce 20% of the results). Busy work is easy to do because unlike prospecting, it's comfortable to do. When you update your website for the fifth time this week, you don't experience rejection. Eventually, you will start to believe that the busy work is important and you'll delude yourself into thinking that you're "working hard." Your lack of production will then no longer be your fault and you can start to identify the usual scapegoats: the market is soft, there's too much competition, your brokerage doesn't provide enough support, etc. Recognize when you're slipping into busy work and be honest with how you're spending your time.

Waking up and making it up – If you don't have a time management plan, you'll have to make it up as you go along. This is probably the number one cause of busy work. Let's see if this sounds familiar: Get up, take a shower, get dressed, stop off on the way to the office and get a latte, go to the office, sit down at your desk, check email and voicemail, get a pad of paper, start a "to do" list for the day. What's wrong with this picture? If you don't already know what you're going to do when you get to the office that day, you're waking up and making it up.

Neglecting pipeline to service current deals – When you get a listing or a hot buyer, you're excited, energized and engaged. When you have multiple deals going on at once, it's a peak, and this peak will tend to take over your life. You know that the only way you'll get paid is if you take your deals all the way through to the close of escrow. There are many action items that need to be performed to make that happen. However, if you spend all of your time on your current deals, you'll hit a valley when they close and you haven't continued to add to your pipeline. Make sure that you carve out time for prospecting even when you're busy with current deals.

Working too much – If you don't work hard, you won't be successful in real estate sales. However, if you work all the time, you'll become less and less effective. This is known as the law of diminishing returns. Human beings need time off to re-charge and rejuvenate. If you neglect this basic human need, you'll inevitably burn out and you'll eventually have to leave the business. Be smart about your scheduling so you get enough sleep and enough time off to be fresh and effective.

Losing control by reacting – Many agents react to every request that comes their way whether from colleagues, brokerage management or clients. If you let others dictate your schedule, you'll lose control of your time, and you won't have time for the activities that produce the results you're seeking. This doesn't mean that you should ignore requests from others; it just means that you need to be in control of your time so you don't spend your day working on the priorities of others.

TIME MANAGEMENT BEST PRACTICES
Having a coherent Time Management Plan will help you to avoid Time Management Traps, and to make intelligent decisions about how you choose to spend your time. The following best practices will help you stay on track with your plan.

Schedule Time Off Annually

Most managing brokers will recommend that you take time off every year. Whether you go on a vacation to an exotic destination, or you take a "staycation" in town, everyone needs time off. I recommend that you plan your time off when you create your business plan toward the end of the current year for the upcoming year. Once you decide when you're going to take time off, put those dates in your calendar, make a commitment to your spouse (if applicable) and inform your managing broker.

It probably makes the most sense to schedule your time off to follow the natural rhythms of the real estate market. In other words, don't schedule a long vacation during the height of the spring selling season. While there are no hard and fast rules, parts of the year when it is best to schedule time off include:

- During the holiday season from Thanksgiving through New Year's Day
- During the summer months when schools are out and many families take vacations
- Over long weekends like Labor Day and Memorial Day when market participants are least active

Treat it Like a Start-up

Most managers will tell you to treat your real estate career like you would if you were in a salaried position. In other words, that you should treat it like a real job where you're expected to show up for work every day, all day and work most of the time while you're there. My advice is slightly different. When you're starting your real estate career, I recommend that you treat it like a start-up.

If you've ever worked in a start-up, you know that you're expected to go beyond the traditional 9am to 5pm work hours. You may end up working extremely long hours while you're ramping up your business. That's just the price of success in real estate sales. You may find that you'll need to work 12 to 14 hours a day six or even seven days a week. You won't, and probably could not, keep up that pace indefinitely. However, at the outset, your commitment will have to be total.

Days of the Week
While you will likely work seven days a week when you are starting your career, you will eventually pare that down so you can maintain your energy and enthusiasm levels and create a sustainable real estate practice. The best days for you to work will be unique to the rhythms of your personal and professional lives. The real estate business is ultimately a weekend-oriented activity as open houses are on weekends, and buyers with "real jobs" are mostly available to view homes on weekends. Therefore, your best candidates for "days off" are during the week.

Here's how you might decide to structure your schedule. In the town where I practice real estate, the broker's tour of new listings occurs on Fridays, so that's automatically a workday. Many brokerage offices hold a weekly sales meeting on a certain day, so you should definitely work on that day. Let's assume that the sales meeting is on Tuesdays.

Mondays are often days that you need to follow up on sales activity that was initiated over the weekend. Assuming you're working on the weekends, that means that your work days so far consist of Saturday, Sunday, Monday, Tuesday and Friday. Wednesday and Thursday are still open.

You might assume, at this point, that you're done as you have boiled it down to two consecutive days off each week. A highly organized real estate professional with an assistant, an escrow coordinator and buyer's agents might be able to take two full days off each week. However, for most agents, the truth is that you'll probably have to work six days a week until you can build such a team.

Assuming that you fit this norm, you should probably work on Thursdays to get ready for the weekend and to prep for any listings that you'll be holding open during the broker's tour on Fridays (again, this is just an example).

So, it looks like Wednesday is your scheduled day off. Hold it sacred and do your best not to let work leak into that day. Inform your managing broker, and your clients. Clients will understand and respect that you have a day off if you inform them about it when you first begin working together. You can also inform people regarding your day off on your voicemail greetings and email out of office notices.

As long as you set the right expectations, you can and should enjoy your day off to the fullest. Remember; when you're off be completely off. Go be with your family, play golf, whatever. No phones, no texts, no emails. This is your time to re-charge.

Protecting Your Calendar
When it comes to how time is spent, there are really only three activities that rise to the level of critical importance: Prospecting, Product Knowledge and Market Knowledge. Make sure that you protect time on your calendar every week for these three activities.

This means that you dedicate uninterrupted time for that activity. In other words, you ensure that nothing encroaches on that time unless there is a true emergency. Consider it like an appointment. When you follow this practice, you protect that time so that you stay focused and consistent.

SAMPLE TIME MANAGEMENT PLAN

The following is a sample Time Management Plan. As stated earlier, your plan will be unique to your individual circumstances. The important thing is to commit the plan to writing and to remain true to it.

Time Management Plan
Scheduled Time Off

- I will take my wife and kids to Disneyland and other vacation spots in Southern California during the week of November 10 through 17
- I will be attending a three day golf outing the weekend of March 15 with my college friends
- I will take the week of the Fourth of July holiday to take my family to a lake house in the Sierra foothills

Days of the week

- I plan to work six days a week
- My work days are Thursday through Tuesday
- Major work activities by day
  - Thursday – Paperwork, Administrative, Creative
  - Friday – Broker Tour and Building Product Knowledge
  - Saturday and Sunday
    - Mornings – Showing Property
    - Afternoons – Open House
  - Monday – Follow up with clients and prospects from the weekend
  - Tuesday – Office Sales Meeting

Non-work Activities – I plan to engage in the following non-work activities

- I will coach my son's soccer team
- I will participate in my weekly referral group
- I will serve on the fundraising committee at my son and daughter's school
- I will play golf on my day off

COMMUNITY INVOLVEMENT

When you think about how you'll spend time outside work, think about how you might be involved in the community. Note that when you are a real estate professional, virtually everything you do can be, or can be perceived to be, a business development activity. It's a fine line to walk to ensure that you're connected socially, spiritually fulfilled and achieving a healthy work-life balance when you're a real estate professional.

Unlike a traditional wage-paid employee of a company, a real estate practitioner carries around his or her work persona everywhere he or she goes. This is one of the key tradeoffs you made when you got into the business. As such, you always have to be prepared to be "on" when someone asks you something real estate-related. This can be at the little league game, after church at the coffee social or during preparations for a school fundraiser.

You can be in denial about this, or you can embrace it is an opportunity. In other words, pursue those activities that are right for your psychological, civic and spiritual enrichment, but be prepared that these activities may produce work-related opportunities. This is nothing to feel guilty about.

On the other hand, if you only pursue these activities to elicit business development opportunities, this will probably backfire. Why? If your intent is not genuine, this will soon become apparent and the people you're trying to cultivate will become cynical and turn away from you.

Also, if your involvement does not come from the heart, you will probably stay with it for a short time and then abandon it due to your lack of interest. This will be a waste of time that you could have spent more productively elsewhere.

Once you decide how you feel about activities outside of work hours, you need to decide whether and how to get involved in the community. As stated earlier, there are limitless opportunities to get involved in civic, religious and philanthropic organizations.

If you are doing it for the right reasons, you might find that your business will benefit from it as well. There are many ways that you can find to be involved in your community:

Affinity – An affinity is any organization to which you have an attachment or association you are proud of. In other words, if you would wear a hat or a sweatshirt with this organization's logo on it, this would be an affinity group for you. This could be an environmental group that advocates for open space and maintains hiking trails, or it could be a pilot's club that attends air shows in your area.

Alumni – Alumni groups are a great way to network with other people and professionals. You may be able to join or create a great referral group; all with the common bond of your high school, college or graduate school that will help you build your business.

Children's Activities – As mentioned earlier, children's activities put you in contact with other parents who are most likely to be at the same life stage as you. This gives you a local network that is socially enriching while keeping you involved in your child's life.

Church – In addition to the spiritual dimension that religious organizations provide they also tend to provide opportunities to serve the community. This will also put you in contact with other generous people with whom you can create meaningful relationships.

Civic – Many real estate agents are also very civic-minded. Perhaps this is because we deal directly with land use issues and property rights on a daily basis. You may find that you gravitate to civic organizations like political parties, trade association, planning commissions, Political Action Committees (PAC), etc. When you join these organizations, you may make a difference in local, regional or even national priorities while you build your contact database.

Community-based – There are many local organizations that provide services to the local community and offer networking opportunities for their members. Examples include service organizations like Rotary and neighborhood organizations that promote community activities like summer Art and Wine festivals.

YOUR BUSINESS PLAN – THE IMPORTANCE OF CONSISTENCY
Now that you've set your Sales Goals, created your Marketing Strategy and identified the necessary Marketing Budget to achieve your sales goals, and developed a Time Management Plan, you need to recognize that the most important aspect of your plan is to remain true to it.

This means that you have to remain consistent despite the inevitable peaks and valleys that occur during the year. This applies to the ups and downs both in your production and in your motivation level. It's easy to get discouraged when things don't go as you planned, or how you wish them to be.

Keep in mind that, all things being equal, the difference between a productive agent and a struggling agent boils down to consistency. If you let your feelings dictate whether you're going to spend the money on that monthly direct mail, or if you decide not to attend your office meeting because you can't summon the motivation to face your colleagues without a sale, you're going to find that lack of consistency becomes a self-fulfilling prophecy.

Many agents quit on their Business Plan just as it is about to bear fruit. They then go on the endless and usually fruitless search for a silver bullet that will save their career. If you let your consistency guard down, you'll likely miss out on what could have been a productive career in real estate sales.

Being consistent in your marketing and prospecting is just like that old saying that if you fail to plan, plan to fail. Only in this case, it's if you fail to be consistent, you will consistently fail in your business. The rest of this section will discuss some of the key activities that will cause your Business Plan to be successful.

Chapter 17 – Winning and Marketing Listings

LISTING PRESENTATIONS

Your listing presentation is your case for why a skeptical homeowner, whom you worked so hard to convert from a lead to a prospect, should hire you to sell their house. The typical seller is interviewing two other agents, their home is their largest asset and the home holds enormous sentimental value. Convincing them to hire you is big time pressure. If you get the listing, you are on your way to a commission check. Perhaps more importantly, you can leverage that listing to get additional listings in your farm.

By the way, there is no greater day than seeing your first sign go up in your farm. It's the real estate equivalent of planting the American flag on the moon. Talk about a giant leap for your career!

Given the importance and significance of this opportunity, you have to walk in with a listing presentation that will give you the best opportunity to win the heart(s) and mind(s) of the homeowner(s) and get the business. In other words, don't wing it and don't use an amateur listing presentation. Not winging it obviously means that you can't show up unprepared. But what is an amateur listing presentation?

An amateur listing presentation is a presentation where the content is either underwhelming or reveals your lack of experience. In other words, if you take the printed marketing collateral from your office and attach a CMA to it and call it a listing presentation, you are guilty of having an amateur listing presentation.

Consumers expect you to have a listing presentation that reflects the quality and inventiveness of the marketing program you will use to sell their home. At this point, if you're not using a laptop or tablet to conduct your listing presentation, you should probably start shopping for one.

There are exceptions to this rule, of course, for agents who are true forces of nature, or established farmers with high name and production recognition. However, for those of us mere mortals who have to work hard to get listings, you must have a digital presentation. This does not mean that you will not bring printed materials to the listing appointment. On the contrary, printed materials will be tangible evidence of the quality of your service delivery, as you will see.

So what goes into your listing presentation? Sellers are really trying to figure out four things from you during the listing presentation:

1. Do you know what you're talking about?
2. Do you know how to sell a home?
3. What do you think their house is worth?
4. Is there a personality fit?

Your presentation should be designed to address these four questions and position you to be selected as the listing agent. Let's look at these points in more detail.

Do you know what you're talking about?
You did something right to get to the table in the first place. You may have been referred, the seller may be an acquaintance or he or she may have contacted you based on your direct marketing program. As such, you already have perceived credibility. The listing presentation is where you convert perceived credibility to actual credibility.

This comes primarily from having and demonstrating confidence, and by communicating a legitimate plan to sell the home. Imagine if you went to a lawyer to do your estate planning and he was nervous, didn't have a firm grasp of the laws affecting your estate and seemed to provide canned responses to your questions. You'd quickly write him off and interview another lawyer.

Similarly, many real estate agents go into a listing presentation nervous, don't do the necessary legwork to know local market conditions and provide scripted answers to questions. True confidence comes from knowing the real estate industry (i.e., laws, MLS rules and local practices), having product knowledge, having market knowledge and practicing scripts for your presentation to the point where your delivery is natural.

Given how important a listing is to your future as a farmer, you need to spend significant time preparing and practicing your listing presentation so your delivery demonstrates that you know what you're talking about.

Do you know how to sell a home?
The best way to convince someone that you can sell a home is to demonstrate that you've done it successfully before. You can use both prior listings and buyer-controlled sales. If you don't have any sales, you will need to focus on the marketing plan that you will use.

Mostly, sellers are looking for a coherent and comprehensive marketing plan for their home. The marketing plan will include some or all of the following elements (include all the things you do for a listing):

Marketing
- Input into MLS
- Listing syndication
- Social media syndication

- Professional photography
- Professional copy writing
- Virtual tour
- Single property websites
- Print ads in area newspaper(s)
- Open house ads in area newspaper(s)
- Just Listed postcards to neighborhood
- Property flyers
- Property signage
- Riders (advertising single property website, text-for-info service, toll-free number for info, etc.)
- Open house directional signs around neighborhood

Sales
- Promote at Association or MLS breakfast meeting
- Promote at broker tour/caravan
- Door knock the neighborhood
- Promote at open house

The more comprehensive the marketing plan, the more compelling it will be to a seller. Think hard about the type of listing agent you want to be, and create a marketing plan that is consistent with your goals. What about expense, you ask? Well, it still takes money to market a home effectively even as more "free" opportunities become available online.

If you don't have, or are unwilling to spend money marketing your listings, you'll never achieve your full potential as a farmer. Remember that it cost you precious funds and/or time to get the opportunity to present your qualifications as a listing agent. If you shortchange your marketing plan, you might be leaving deals on the table.

What do you think my house is worth?
Sometimes it's easy to think that sellers only care about two things: What their house is worth, and your commission rate. While the market determines what their house is worth, you

determine what your commission rate will be. If you can demonstrate that you know what you're talking about, that you have an effective marketing plan and that you are easy to get along with, the pressure on your commission rate will ease. When all is said and done, people are willing to pay a fair price for something of value. Your job is to demonstrate your value so you can maintain your commission levels.

The real question comes down to what their house is "worth." Unlike 100 share of GE stock, a home has no such "correct" market value. Remember that your job is not to be an appraiser. You should not spend an inordinate amount of time analyzing comparables to come up with the most statistically supported opinion of value.

This is not to say that you should ignore comparables. You have to do the research that is required for you to have an informed opinion regarding the home's worth. The point is that there is no prize for having the most accurate opinion of value.

A home is only worth what a qualified buyer is willing to pay for it at a specific point in time. What the seller probably doesn't realize is that when they ask you what their home is worth, they're really asking you what the list price should be. Your job is to develop a pricing strategy that helps the seller achieve their goal.

That is why you should avoid providing a definitive answer to the question of what their house is worth. Always try to talk in ranges, and be sure that the seller understands that you'll only control the list price, not what buyers are willing to pay for the home. When you work with comparables, discuss them as a guide to help inform your pricing strategy.

Your pricing strategy is something that you can talk about during the listing presentation. However, you should attempt to delay the actual decision of a specific list price to the point where you put the listing on the market. Why? Because you will need to take a fresh look at the comparables and ascertain the state of the market at that point in time. Only then should you commit to the list price.

If pressed, you can say something like, "Well, if we were to put the home on the market this afternoon, I would probably recommend a list price $398,000. However, things can change dramatically in the real estate market, even over a short period of time. When we put the home on the market, I will provide you with an updated CMA, and we will make the decision at that time." You don't want to come across as evasive, but do your best not to get pinned down to specific numbers before you're ready.

The list price is influenced by market conditions and by the seller(s) personal situation and timeframe. To find out how the seller's personal situation will influence the pricing strategy, you will need to do some basic discovery. Probe for answers to questions like (Note – this is not an exhaustive list):

1. How quickly do you need to sell?
2. How much equity do you think you have in your home?
3. What are you going to do after you sell this home?
4. What will you use the money for?
5. How many stakeholders will be involved in the decision to sell?

Keep in mind that these issues tend to be very personal. As such, you probably won't be able to come out and ask them like a reporter. You'll need to work them into the discussion so that it seems more conversational.

The value of knowing this information is very important. Let me give you an example. Suppose you had a listing presentation involving a home that was owned by the same family for more than 30 years. The wife and husband raised their family in the home, but now both parents have passed away (the husband passed way 12 years ago and the wife recently passed away).

The five surviving siblings are now selling the home and they will split the proceeds evenly. The eldest son is representing the other siblings and he says that he is extremely busy, and he's also coming from out of town to handle the sale, so he'd like to sell as quickly as possible. As the proceeds from the house are being split five ways, the price they get for the house does not impact any one of the siblings dramatically. This situation would lead you to conclude that the pricing strategy should be aggressive to sell the home quickly.

As this example demonstrates, the personal situation of the seller(s) often has as much to do with pricing strategy as do market conditions. Do your best to discover the specific situation of each seller.

Finally, be aware that some agents will try to get listings by telling the seller that their home is worth more than its actual market value. They think that by agreeing to a high list price, they can make a price adjustment later and still sell the house.

I caution against using this strategy in your practice, as it is the number one cause of expired and cancelled listings. Overpriced listings will consume your financial resources and your time, and you only get paid when your transactions close. So, make sure your listings have a legitimate shot of crossing the finish line.

Is there a personality fit?
At the end of the day, most real estate professionals who get to a listing appointment will offer great service and compelling

marketing plans. Often, the decision comes down to the person that the seller likes the most. This doesn't necessarily mean that the most gregarious agent will get the listing. If the seller is extremely analytical, they may prefer the soft-spoken agent who can speak at length regarding market trends and statistics. It all comes down to personality fit.

So how can you ensure that you'll be perceived as the best fit? This requires some keen observation and adaptability on your part. When you meet with the seller(s), try to ascertain what they are like. Are they introverted? Are they excitable? Are they reserved? Are they expressive? Are they analytical? People have a tendency to want to work with service providers who are most like themselves.

If you can determine the type of personality they have, you can emphasize those traits in yourself and your delivery. This doesn't mean that you should be phony. Of course, you need to be yourself. We're talking about making subtle changes to best position you as the person they want to work with. Also, keep in mind that an introvert may be looking for the "Super Salesman" type. It's all about reading the person, the situation and the verbal and non-verbal cues and then adapting so that they see you as the best fit.

The other approach to finding fit is to find common ground. The easiest way to do this is to engage in small talk and ask questions to see if you have anything in common. This could be that you're both from the same region of the country, lived in the same area, previously worked in the same industry, went to the same college (or rival college), attend the same church, have/had kids in the same school, follow the same sports team, etc. Once you have this common foundation, it's easier to build a strong relationship.

HOW TO HANDLE LISTING APPOINTMENTS

Once you've built up your confidence through product knowledge, market knowledge and by practicing your listing presentation, you're ready to go on a listing appointment. There are many schools of thought on how to handle listing appointments.

For example, some brokers counsel that listing appointments should be handled in two separate meetings. The first meeting is for you to meet the seller and tour the house. Once you have this information, you go back and complete the CMA that you present at the second meeting.

I am not a proponent of the two step approach because most homeowners find it too cumbersome, it doubles your effort on the listing and it forces you to be very precise regarding the value of the house (because now that you've seen it, you better have a specific answer). You should do whatever you think will be most effective for you, but I will lay out a plan for a single listing appointment that has worked for me, and you can either follow it entirely or tweak it to fit your style.

BEFORE THE LISTING APPOINTMENT

I keep a checklist that I use to make sure I do everything I need to get ready for a listing appointment.

Take a Photo of the House – Before the listing appointment, I take a photo of the house. I then use this in my presentation, my CMA and in sample marketing materials. To avoid the "creep" factor when they see their house in your materials, I always tell the seller when I'm setting the appointment that I'll be driving by to preview the home and to take a subject property photo.

Access Property Profile – Usually available from county records, you should download the property profile that gives you property information (bedrooms, bathrooms, square footage, etc.), title information and information regarding any liens on the property. You will need this for your CMA, but it also gives you other pertinent information about the house (like the fact that the person who called you to sell the house doesn't have an ownership interest in the house).

Prepare CMA – Put together a professional CMA that can be easily interpreted by a layperson. Make sure that your CMA allows for a range estimate of value. The script that I use for the CMA is something like the following, "The CMA I put together gives you an approximation of your home's value based on market statistics for homes like yours. As I've never seen the inside of your home before today, it does not include adjustments for the specific features and condition of your home. Also, home values are very dynamic and the range estimate I've given you is what the market would seem to support today. Before we would put the home on the market, I would create a new report to see how market conditions would affect the list price. You can look at the report in more detail at your convenience and call me with any questions you may have."

Customize Listing Presentation – While I have a standard listing presentation, I always customize it for every listing appointment. This includes obvious changes like the seller's name(s) and their property's information, and subtle changes based on the individuals involved and the location of the home. When you understand the key questions sellers are looking to answer, you can create a winning listing presentation. Your listing presentation will be unique to you, your local market, your marketing program and the specific benefits of your brokerage firm.

However you structure it, it must address the following:

- Your background, expertise, accomplishments and proof of production
- The benefits of working with your brokerage firm
- The marketing program you will employ to sell their house
- A range estimate of what you think their home is worth and a discussion of how you would price it

Neighborhood Information/Guest Book Binder – A good way to demonstrate local market knowledge is to bring a binder that includes information about the local neighborhood: Census information, schools, restaurants, parks, shopping, regional amenities, history, etc. Also, you should include a Guest Registry that you can use to record contact information from potential buyers at an open house. Tell the seller that you would leave the binder at the home to provide buyers with information regarding local amenities and to capture buyer leads.

Assemble Listing Package (Bound) – The listing package is the printed piece that you will leave behind with the seller. The listing package includes information about you, your brokerage, the CMA, sample marketing materials, your business card, etc.

Bring Completed Listing Agreement – Like a boy scout, you should always be prepared. In this case, you need to be prepared to close the deal. At some point in the conversation, when you sense things are going well, you can bring out the listing agreement and ask them to sign. A typical script for this would be something like, "I think we've covered all the important aspects of my services, so if you sign the listing agreement today, I can get started on this program right away. Let's go over the main points of the agreement."

This is known as the assumptive close. You want to be assertive without being pushy. If a seller is ready to sign after your listing presentation, don't introduce an unnecessary delay by having to come back with a listing agreement. This will give them time to think about it and possibly change their mind. Having a completed listing agreement also projects that you are thorough and prepared.

Write Thank You Note - As you're putting together the rest of your listing materials, go ahead and write thank you letter thanking the seller for the opportunity to present your marketing program. Mail it the day of your listing appointment, if possible, but don't mail it until you actually have the appointment to avoid embarrassment (e.g., a last minute re-schedule). Yes, a physical thank you note is old school, and yes, it will be noticed and appreciated by your potential client.

Now that you have all your listing material prepared, it's time to go to the appointment. I think it goes without saying that you must dress professionally for the listing appointment. This is true even if this is an acquaintance because you want them to know that you are a real professional and you don't take their business for granted. Close friends and family are a different matter, so you have to play those by ear.

It would also seem to go without saying that you should show up on time. However, do not knock on the door early. I suggest getting to the appointment at lease five minutes early. You can stay in your car and get your things ready. When you're ready, walk up to the door and knock right when the appointed time arrives. This will demonstrate to your potential clients that you are organized, prompt and courteous by not showing up early.

While you're waiting for the door to be answered, remember the importance of this meeting. Take a deep breath. Stand up straight. Hold your briefcase in your left hand (so you can shake hands when they open the door). I suggest that you do not look into the house through a window or even look straight at the door. This could make the homeowner uncomfortable. Look off to the side like you're thinking about something important. When the door opens, look to the homeowner, smile broadly, extend your hand, and say, "You must be Jim. Steve Elich, pleasure to meet you." It's show time!

DURING THE LISTING APPOINTMENT

Now that you're in the prospect's home, the importance of everything you do is magnified. They'll be watching you intently to listen to your answers, and to read your body language. Again, it's all about confidence. If you've done your homework, everything will be fine. How the appointment is structured is almost always up to you. The seller will be looking for you to take the lead. This is no time to be passive. Take the reins and watch the seller become relieved that they don't have to lead the meeting.

The first thing I do when I arrive at a listing appointment is to thank the seller for inviting me to come to their house to present your marketing program. The second thing I do is ask the seller if all the decision makers are present (you should pre-qualify this when you set the appointment). The third thing I ask is if they have any time constraints. The typical listing presentation takes about two hours, so if they have another agent coming in an hour, for example, I want to know about it up front.

Once I have those basic logistics covered, I tell them that I'd like to tour the house with them so that I can take notes about the home. Tell the seller that you will use this information to refine your CMA and in the marketing materials you produce (planting the seeds for the assumptive close). Have them take you around the house and ask them to point out things that they particularly like about the house or that they think would be good selling points. Use a notepad or electronic device to take notes.

Pay the homeowner compliments about their home. Virtually everyone has pride of ownership in their home and making them feel good about their home will transfer positive feelings to you. Use this time to build rapport with the client, to probe to understand their situation better and to demonstrate your product knowledge (e.g., "I'd say roughly half of the homes in this subdivision have converted the patio area into a sun room like was done here. Did you do the work?").

When the tour is complete, thank the seller for the information. Tell them that at this point you'd like to present information about your services. I avoid sitting on sofas or easy chairs. Ask to sit at the dining table. You should be using your laptop or tablet, so sitting at a table will help facilitate your presentation. Make sure your presentation is accessible quickly. Bring it up and get ready to present. Use a professional style, but make sure that you allow for interaction and questions.

As you go through your presentation, pause frequently to ask if the seller has any questions and to ask probing questions of your own. Probing questions help you better understand the seller's situation and motivational factors. An example of a probing question would be, "So, have you been considering selling for a long time, or is this more recent?"

During your presentation, you should do your best to mirror the behavior of the sellers. For example, if they are talkative and they're being chatty, don't insist on plowing through your presentation uninterrupted. It is far better to build rapport than to get your points across in your preferred style. This does not mean that you should acquiesce to the seller to the point where they control the appointment. However, people generally have a more favorable opinion about someone when they are more like themselves.

As you get close to the end of your presentation, you should be able to gauge whether you are building the type of rapport that will enable you to close the deal on the spot. Make sure that you phrase things in the assumptive format. For example, "When we order the inspections, will you want to be there?" When you get to the end of your presentation and there are no further questions, you need to ask for the business.

You will have to develop your own style and approach, but you can start with something like, "So if there are no more questions, I'd like to go over the listing agreement with you now." Another approach is, "So if I've answered all of your questions, is there any reason why you wouldn't be able to sign the listing agreement today?" By phrasing this as a question, it will force your potential client to respond.

DON'T SAY ANYTHING UNTIL THEY RESPOND! It's conventional wisdom in sales that the first person to talk when you ask a question "loses." In other words, if you wait for them to respond, they have to give a response that either gets you the business, or prompts them to come up with a condition for you to get the business. For example, their response might be, "Well, we liked your presentation, but we still have to interview one more agent." Now you know what you have to overcome to get the business. In effect, you've "won."

However, if you respond after you first ask the question, it weakens your position. For example, "So if I've answered all of your questions, is there any reason why you wouldn't be able to sign the listing agreement today?" Pause. "Because if there's anything else you need to know, I can go over that now." Now the seller has to come up with something like, "No, I think you covered it fairly well. We'll think about it and let you know." See the difference?

Assuming they don't agree to sign the listing agreement right away, the sellers' response will tell you what objection you will need to overcome to get the listing. The two most common responses are that they need to think about it, or that they're still interviewing other agents. How you respond depends on your style. If they tell you they need to think about it, ask them what it is they need to think about and attempt to overcome the objection.

You can probe to determine what the real issue might be, but the more you push a decision when they are not ready, the less likely you will be to get the listing. Once you've exhausted all of your opportunities to close the business, ask your prospects when they plan to make a decision. At that point, thank them for the appointment, and politely excuse yourself from their home.

AFTER THE LISTING APPOINTMENT
Once you've completed the listing appointment, send the sellers the thank you card you prepared before the listing appointment. Also, provide any follow-up that you promised before or during the listing appointment. Finally, check in with the sellers on the date you agreed to follow up with them. Beyond these basics, there is little you can do at this point to secure the listing. Being diligent about following up and being available to the sellers is your best course of action.

Now that the listing appointment is over, you need to move on to new business. Keep your prospecting going, and continue to service your existing clients. Do not become obsessed with the listing, especially if it goes to someone else. You're not going to win all the listings for which you interview. Accept this as a fact of life and move on. Bitterness at not being chosen is not only counterproductive, but also typically unwarranted. The sellers almost certainly have nothing against you, so try not to take it personally if you're not chosen.

The only time to be truly concerned is if you generate lots of listing appointments and you are never, or rarely, chosen. This is a sign that your listing presentation may not be compelling, or that your delivery is lacking in some way. If this is the case, your best option is to present to a colleague in your office or your managing broker to see if something is amiss.

When you do get that wonderful call that you've been selected to represent the seller in the sale of their home, allow yourself some time to celebrate and acknowledge your success. Then get down to the business of promoting the listing to generate a commission check and, more importantly, to leverage that listing into more business. The topic of marketing a listing is big enough to warrant its own book. As this book is focused on Farming, suffice it to say that you should make sure to promote your new listing to your farm audience. Proof of production remains the best way to generate additional business and referrals.

Chapter 18 – How to Conduct an Open House

Like working with scripts, conducting an open house is something that you need to make your own. Each agent will have a different style and different techniques. The following abbreviated primer will help get you going in the right direction:

Put your open house signs out in the morning – Open house signs are the most cost-effective marketing tools available to you. These signs are like small billboards that promote you for free (excluding your initial cost to buy them, your time to put them out and your gas, of course). Even better, you can put these miniature billboards all around your farm where they demonstrate your proof of production and marketing ability. The best practice I know of regarding signs is as follows.

Order signs that have your open house hours printed on them. Get up early the day of your open house and put the signs out before the morning rush begins. This way, you're not confusing anyone because your hours are posted, but you get the benefit of having the signs out all day. A secondary benefit of this tactic is that you won't be scrambling to put the signs out on your way to the open house. Be sure to check with your municipality to make sure you comply with all signage ordinances before you put your signs out.

Door knock around the listing – A listing is something you need to sell to get paid, but it also valuable as a prospecting tool. The best way to get to know the neighbors in your farm is to invite them to the open house. This is a very non-intrusive form of door knocking. Take flyers with you, invite them to come to the open house and then ask them if they know of anyone thinking of moving into the neighborhood. This will spark a conversation that could lead to referral opportunities. Also, your diligence in actively seeking buyers for the property will make a good impression on these future sellers.

Take the flyers out of the flyer box – If the yard sign has a flyer box, make sure that you remove the flyers during the open house. This prevents potential buyers from just picking up the flyer and driving off. At least make them come inside to get the flyer!

Make sure the house is presentable – Let's face it, some sellers just can't keep a home in open house form. Coach your clients as best you can, but part of selling real estate is making sure that the home appears in its best light. If that means getting the broom out and sweeping the crumbs off the kitchen floor, so be it. Remember that the condition and presentation of the property affects your ability to sell it and is a direct reflection of you as an agent.

Turn on all the lights – Homes show better when the lights are turned on. This holds true for both photography and an open house.

Turn on music – I find that having music on during an open house provides a level of ambience that makes buyers feel more comfortable. If you have a tentative buyer and they walk into a quiet house and the only sound is the creaking of the floorboards, this could make for an awkward encounter. Better to have some uplifting, yet professional musical accompaniment. If your seller does not have appropriate musical equipment, bring your own.

Overcome negative auditory or odor deficiencies – If you have an obvious auditory deficiency like traffic noise, try to come up with ways to minimize its negative effect. Similarly, if there is a source of unpleasant odor, do something to mask it like scented candles or more aggressive ventilation. There'll be time to disclose the sources of these issues later; you want potential buyers to fall in love with the place first.

Greeting open house guests – There are many philosophies regarding how to handle guests at an open house. They range from an agent I know who advocates saying, "Come in, have a look around and let me know if you have any questions," to agents who require registration before they provide the guest with a property flyer. I try to keep in mind the two goals I have for an open house. Number one is to sell the property.

Number two is to leverage the listing to get more business and referrals. I find that the best approach is to build rapport with guests by asking some non-threatening introductory questions about their housing search, and then casually probing further to see if they are a fit as a potential client.

Always make neighbors feel welcome, as they are your potential future clients. They'll come to the open house and say things like, "We're just neighbors," "We're just looky-loos," or "We're just nosy neighbors." My standard response is, "Neighbors are always welcome at my open house. How long have you lived in the neighborhood?"

Capturing contact information – Unless you want to collect the contact information of everyone who visits your open house so you can put them on some type of drip marketing program, you'll probably only capture the contact information of guests with whom you've developed rapport or specific follow-up action items.

Make sure that you have some organized system for gathering contact information that looks professional and that is easy for you to manage when you get back to your office. Be sure to take copious notes about your possible client to jog your memory when you follow up. By the way, the best way to get someone's phone number is to ask, "And what is the best number to reach you?"

Providing the seller with an open house report – Your seller will be very anxious to know how the open house went. Make sure that you keep track of the number of parties that visited the open house so you can provide the sellers with this information. You can also give the seller some commentary about the contacts you made, but be sure not to raise their expectations just to make the open house seem more promising than it was.

If necessary, provide your clients with any feedback from guests that might help them come to terms with pricing or property condition issues. The open house report is just another way for you to keep the lines of communication with your client open and constructive.

Part 4 – Reviewing Your Farming Performance

"Whether you think you can or think you can't - you are right."

—— Henry Ford

If you follow the frameworks and fundamentals outlined in this book, you should be in a position to outperform your peers. If things are going well, you'll want to adjust your forecasting and your farming practices to reflect and build on your success. If you're not attaining your goals, you'll want to review your performance and determine how you can increase your odds of success.

I suggest that you review your performance at least quarterly to see if you are on track to meet your sales goals, and to monitor your budget to make sure you're not digging yourself a big hole. However, on an annual basis, you need to take a step back and perform a comprehensive review of your farming operation. This section helps you answer the important questions that you should ponder as you assess your performance.

Chapter 19 – Key Farming Evaluation Questions

There are some key questions you should ask yourself about your farming performance. Read these questions before you start farming and then again after a year of farming. These questions will help do some deep thinking regarding your farming performance, how to improve your operation and whether you should continue farming.

Am I achieving my annual sales goals?
The first and most important area to investigate is whether you're achieving your annual sales goals. When you're having a good year, reviewing your sales performance is fun. If you're not achieving your sales targets, the review can be very sobering. If you're achieving your sales goals, you are in a great position.

The toughest question your can ask yourself is whether you set the bar too low. Be honest with yourself. If your goals are easily attainable, you're not stretching yourself as much as you should. Moreover, as you achieve success, you'll want to increase your sales goals because your market share should grow as your brand builds.

If you're partly achieving your goals, you'll have to look at the trends and determine if you're farming is moving in the right direction. If you had some early success because you knew people in your farm who were ready to sell, but activity has fallen off, the trend line is not favorable.

Alternately, if you plodded along for several months with seemingly nothing to show for it, then got some phone calls for information or assistance and later got invited to listing presentations, your trends are moving in the right direction. If you're starting to get calls that start with, "I know you specialize in this area…", or "You must handle a lot of the business in the area…" you know that your farming program is beginning to take root. Take heart and keep going, success is coming if you stick with it.

On the other hand, if you're falling well short of your goals, you're not getting any responses to your direct marketing program and you are not getting any calls after a year of activity, you need to give your farming an honest assessment. In finance, there's a concept called "sunk cost." This term refers to money (and time) that you've already spent. As you can't recover it, these resources are "sunk" like a ship at the bottom of the ocean.

The concept is that you shouldn't expend new resources to justify sunk costs or previous "investments" in your farm if your farm is fundamentally broken in some way. However, you should know that just when many farmers are about to start seeing success, they lose heart and give up. Look hard for positive signs of traction before throwing in the towel on your existing farm.

Do I forecast future success in my farm?

If you haven't been achieving your sales goals, but you are starting to see the telltale signs of success, you probably should continue your farming program. What are the telltale signs of success? These include, but are not limited to:

- Responses to your direct mail program calls to action
- Emails and calls from homeowners asking for various forms of advice and assistance (e.g., "Do you know of a good plumber?")
- Comments from neighbors, friends and area residents that they're "getting your stuff" in the mail, seeing your ads in the paper or seeing you online
- Invitations for listing appointments

- People doing double takes when they recognize you at a local store or eatery

You may see other signs that are unique to your particular situation. These are signs that your marketing is taking root and that success is coming. If you can persevere through this period, you may be able to forecast future success in your farm. Review your business plan to identify ways that you might be able to increase your odds of success.

Is there a fundamental shift occurring in my farm?
Sometimes, changes to the basic underpinnings of a farm begin to take place. On the one hand, you might be experiencing a trend that positively affects your farm. For example, the schools in your farm may be improving and increasing the value of the homes in your farm territory. This increased demand usually means that your commissions will be going up with the value of the homes, and homes will sell more quickly.

On the other hand, you might be experiencing a trend that negatively affects your farm. For example, the loss of a major local employer to another state or country might lead to decreased demand for housing and, therefore, lower prices. Inventory might build and become harder to sell. This will affect both your commission levels and your time-to-commission.

As you identify these fundamental shifts in your farm, you will have to determine whether and how to react. Every challenge is a potential opportunity, as those who focused on REOs early on in the housing crisis aptly demonstrate.

Recognize that even a seemingly positive trend like improving schools could have negative consequences, like increased farming competition. Also be sure to separate structural changes (the loss of manufacturing jobs) from seasonal or cyclical fluctuations.

Should I increase or decrease the size of my farm?

After you've farmed your area for certain amount of time, you may decide that you either want to increase the size of your farm, or go the other way and decrease it. Many factors would enter into the decision to modify the size of the farm. For example, if there is an adjacent area that you've long wanted to add, but were waiting for a certain amount of sales in your original farm to fund the expansion, you might be at a point where you are ready to add the adjacent area.

Alternatively, you might be in a scenario in which you've had some success, but you feel that you will be more successful if you mail more often. In this case, you might consider reducing your farm size and increasing the number of mailings you send. Many farmers have cut their farm in half and mailed twice as often to jump-start their farm. You can always increase your farm later when you've achieved a sustainable level of success.

Should I change my focus to a new farm area?

If you've had negative experiences in your existing farm, or insufficient activity in your farm, it doesn't necessarily mean that you're not a good farmer. As I can personally attest, you can abandon a farm where you've struggled and go on to be a productive farmer in another area.

My original farm made me miserable, wasn't close to my house and there was a fundamental shift underway (away from full service to limited service brokerages). Therefore, it was a bad fit for me. My new farm is close to my house and it has paid-off financially. You can recover from a bad farm, but it is a decision that should not be taken lightly.

You should go through the entire evaluation process of Part 2 and the business plan section of Part 3 for your new farm before making this type of change. Also, should have decent product and market knowledge in your prospective farm before making the switch.

How can I improve my revenue drivers?
When you are actively working a farm, there are several drivers that determine how much revenue you are able to generate. The revenue drivers include the following. If you are looking to improve your revenue performance, you need to identify how you can influence these drivers.

Number of Homes in Farm – If you increase the size of your potential market, you increase the revenue potential of the farm. Of course, you also increase the expense profile of the farm for variable expenses like direct mail (fixed expenses like print ads are less expensive per prospect for larger farms).

Market Share – To a large degree, the amount of market share you get in your farm is a function of your effort in converting prospects into clients. If you are more aggressive than other agents in asking for referrals, following up on leads, door knocking and sending direct mail, you can and will increase your market share. You can also do things like role-play your listing presentation to increase your win rate. Sending direct mail and sitting back is not farming, and it won't maximize your market share.

Average Commission Rate – The amount that you get paid by sellers in your farm is a matter of negotiation. The better you are able to communicate and demonstrate your value proposition, the more likely you will be to charge higher rates for your service. Moreover, the higher your production level in your farm, the more confidence sellers will have in you and they will be less likely to push back on your commission rate.

Commission Split – This is often a sensitive topic with your managing broker and/or your brokerage firm as the money they get on the commissions split is how they keep the doors open and the lights on. Remember that your firm has to make money to provide you with a brand, a place to conduct business, management support, marketing support, etc. Having said that, the better your commission split, the more revenue that accrues to you personally. If you are generating production in your farm, your split will likely improve based on your production level without having to negotiate for a higher split. If you are looking to negotiate a higher split, one of the best ways to convince your firm to give you a higher split is the financial commitment you are making to your farm.

What can I do to maintain a positive attitude?

Farming is a long-range activity. For even the most successful agents, there are sure to be times when frustration, fatigue and angst begin to take their toll. You may go through periods where you're getting lots of calls, appointments and listings. Everything is clicking. Then, seemingly for no reason, your sales pipeline begins to run dry.

Often, you are just living through a temporary dry spell. We live in an inter-connected, unpredictable world where most of the variables are out of our control. Remember that maintaining a positive attitude during one of these dry spells is one of the things within your control. Take this time to re-double your prospecting, catch up on deferred projects and even to take some extra time off.

If you maintain your professionalism and maintain a positive attitude, you should make it through the dry spell and enjoy the fruits of a full pipeline again.

Am I having fun faming my farm?

Do you like your farm? Do you enjoy driving through it, or going for a jog through it? Do you get along with the people who live in your farm? Do you enjoy having an open house and meeting the neighbors? Do you like thinking about your farm when you're at the office? Do you like touring the homes in your farm to increase your product knowledge? Do you mind reading market statistics about your farm, or calling agents to find out how many offers that recently sold house received?

Alternatively, is your farm making you miserable? Do you dread the thought of driving to it? Do you make up excuses to avoid touring properties there? Do you cringe when a "nosy neighbor" is coming up the walk to your open house? Are you falling behind in your market knowledge in the farm? Do you daydream about other prospecting methods?

Whether your farm is making you happy or driving you nuts, you should pay attention to your feelings about your farm. If you're happy farming your farm, your likelihood of success is much higher. Common sense dictates that you'll put more and better effort into an activity you enjoy.

If your farm or farming makes you fundamentally unhappy, it is unlikely that you'll be able to overcome your emotions to achieve long-term success. Be honest with yourself and take your emotions into consideration when evaluating whether and how to farm.

Am I a Farmer?
At the end of the day, you have to ask yourself the fundamental question, "Am I a farmer?" Remember that farming is something that takes time, discipline and resources. There are many ways to create a successful real estate practice and farming is just one of them. If your talents are better suited to another prospecting method, you should embrace that strategy wholeheartedly.

If you decide to be a farmer for the long haul, I wish you all the best. I hope this book has provided you with knowledge and frameworks that you can use to achieve success. Regardless of how you decide to build your real estate practice, I wish you nothing but financial success, professional fulfillment and much happiness in your business and personal relationships.

94959759R10080

Made in the USA
Middletown, DE
23 October 2018